SECRET BARNARD CASTLE & TEESDALE

Andrew Graham Stables

AMBERLEY

In memory of Harry Stables (1930–87)

First published 2018

Amberley Publishing
The Hill, Stroud
Gloucestershire, GL5 4EP

www.amberley-books.com

Copyright © Andrew Graham Stables, 2018

The right of Andrew Graham Stables to be identified as the Author of this work has been asserted in accordance with the Copyrights, Designs and Patents Act 1988.

ISBN 978 1 4456 7326 4 (print)
ISBN 978 1 4456 7327 1 (ebook)

British Library Cataloguing in Publication Data.
A catalogue record for this book is available from the British Library.

Origination by Amberley Publishing.
Printed in Great Britain.

Contents

Introduction

Teesdale is part of the second largest designated Area of Outstanding Natural Beauty in England and Wales, and is a valley named after the river coursing through it. Teesdale encompasses Cross Fell (the highest peak in the Pennines), Middleton-in-Teesdale, Barnard Castle and through to Gainford. The area includes Hamsterley to the north and Bowes to the south, but these borders were created by government changes in 1974. The River Tees is the traditional border between Yorkshire and Durham, but the reality is the people from either side of this natural boundary have always been intrinsically connected by geography, culture and language.

At its border is an enormous ancient British fortified city, once ruled by a queen who chose the path of co-operation rather than opposition to the Roman invaders. The pre-Roman peoples left significant evidence of their existence throughout the Dale, including mystical burial grounds, hilltop forts and simpler domestic dwellings. Though co-operation may have been their first defence from the Mediterranean aggressors, this changed as the imperialists reached further north and the land was exploited by the Romans.

Teesdale is located between Weardale and Swaledale.

The ancient route and Roman road into Teesdale – now the A66.

Hordes of invaders from the east followed the abandonment of Britannia by the Romans. The Picts, Saxons and Scotti began to raid the country and many would settle the fertile areas. This opened up the floodgates to further settlement by the Jutes, Angles and Frisians who came from the north coast of Europe. It is still strongly debated whether or not the new settlers squeezed out or killed the indigenous people – even the genetic evidence is unclear. Whatever the reality of the local inhabitants' origins, within 400 years the region was affected by a new threat: the Vikings, who dominated the region for the next 200 years. But perhaps the Norman invaders had the most significant influence on the area, with the creation of several castles and one family member giving their name to Barnard Castle. They became the ruling classes and their descendants still have an influence on the area to this day. The natural resources of the Pennines have been stripped from the land for centuries and are particularly famous for lead, with the establishment of the London Lead Co. Northern Headquarters at Middleton-in-Teesdale in 1815.

There is a vast amount of history contained within its picturesque valleys, which has attracted many writers and artists over the years. Sir Walter Scott hid in a secret cave by the River Greta to pen some of his verses, Charles Dickins took inspiration for his books following a visit, and one of our greatest artists – J. M. W Turner – produced some of his finest work depicting Teesdale.

There was a king of Scotland who was born in England at Barnard Castle and Richard III left a permanent legacy in the town, but did he also ensconce the murderer of the princes in the Dale? Churchill also visited the area to inspect some secret operations being carried out prior to D-Day and only fragments remain of the Queen Mother's childhood castle. Add to this one of the finest museums in the North (built in the style of a French chateau), the largest waterfall in England, and villages lost under reservoirs and you will be surprised at the secrets Teesdale will unveil.

The Roman road from Bowes to Binchester that crosses the River Tees below Barnard Castle – now the A67.

Looking from Lunedale towards the Yorksire Dales.

1. Natural Beauty

The Sleepy Sheep and Other Glacial Features

On the banks of the River Tees, heading upstream towards Towler Hill out of Barnard Castle, is a glacial erratic of pink Shap granite. Known as the Sleepy Sheep, this is a rock deposited by the vast glacial sheet that once covered northern Britain. This natural feature could easily be mistaken for a sheep asleep in the field.

There are many erratics in Teesdale, with the largest being the Great Stone in Deepdale. Another, called the South Park Stone, was deposited in the bed of the River Tees approximately 300 yards upstream of Winston Bridge before being moved again in 1900, 10 miles further east to its current location in the park at Darlington. Other unusual stones include the Robin Hood's Stone in Lunedale, just above Selset Reservoir, and the Scotsmans Stone on the Greta, made famous in a painting by John Sell Cotman.

Teesdale is rich with glacial features including drumlins, glacial deposits, ridges, channels and moraines. In Upper Teesdale – especially around Harwood – there is a series of drumlins, which manifest as smooth uniform hillocks and as you cross from Cotherstone up to Romaldkirk, after the Hunderthwaite turn off, is a moraine that was deposited during the last ice age – around 10–12,000 years ago.

The Sleepy Sheep.

Robin Hood's Stone, Lunedale.

DID YOU KNOW?
Egglestone marble (also known as Teesdale marble) from the Egglestone Abbey area was used to make fonts in Barnard Castle, Kendal, Richmond and Yarm, as well as fine tombs in York.

Teesdale Reservoirs

At the beginning of the nineteenth century, Teesside was thirsty for water, which was necessary for the ever-growing industries, and Pennine dams were regarded as a 'natural' solution. Between 1840 and 1970 over 200 were built in the Pennines to supply the industries of Manchester, Leeds, Sheffield and Teesside. There were clear advantages when supplying water from upland areas. where high rainfall, natural river courses and gravity could be used to transport this vital commodity.

McCulloch concludes that the dams in Teesdale were influenced by politics as much as the location, and the first dams could be built in the area due to the increased wealth of the urban industrialists. They bargained with an almost feudal society of aristocratic Pennine landowners and their small tenant farmers, who had few resources and very little power to stop 'progress'. In the late nineteenth century permission to build dams could be easily negotiated with the gentry, but later – certainly post-Second World War – opposition grew from a people who cared for the countryside.

Reservoir	Engineer	Year Opened	River	Volume
Hury	J. Mansergh	1894	Balder	3.9 Mm^3
Blackton	J. Mansergh	1896	Balder	2.1 Mm^3
Grassholme	E. Mansergh	1914	Lune	6.1 Mm^3
Selset	J. Mansergh	1959	Lune	15.3 Mm^3
Balderhead	J. Mansergh	1964	Balder	19.7 Mm^3
Green	M. Kennard	1970	Tees	40.9 Mm^3

When Selset Reservoir was built in 1959 several farms were sunk below the water, including The Slack, where my maternal grandmother was born. Other farms lost include Thwaites, Bink House, Turner Holme, High Selset, Low Wemmergill and Blake House.

Grassholme Reservoir.

Selset Reservoir.

The reservoirs were built on tributaries of the rivers Tees, Balder and Lune, but this changed in 1970 with the construction of Cow Green Reservoir, which was built near to the source of the Tees. Cow Green took three years to build and cost around £2.5 million, even though the site above Cauldron Snout had originally been deemed unsuitable by earlier surveys. The reservoir regulates the water into the River Tees and maintains the flow during dry periods. Equally, during times of flooding the reservoir holds water, and has effectively removed the threat of what was known as the 'Tees Bore'. The Bore was a sudden flood of water described by one commentator as:

> But a thin and narrow stream on dry summer days, but in times of rain it broadens and swells with an amazing suddenness rushing downwards with a great roar and tumult of waters, so unexpected, sometimes and with a character so much resembling the opposite phenomenon of the bore on the Severn, that holiday visitors, in apprehensive of calamity, have before now been carried headlong over the terrible cataract of High Force.

Cow Green Reservoir is still regarded by some 'as an unforgivable intrusion' (Ratcliffe, 2000) and the loss of 'valued vegetation' that was drowned under this industrial lake. Others might say they add to the beauty of the Dale, as bodies of water often do, reflecting and enhancing the countryside.

Cow Green Reservoir.

High Force.

God's Bridge, Near Bowes

Heading west from Bowes, around 2 miles along the River Greta, is a natural limestone bridge called God's Bridge. This is where the softer rock from below the harder rock has dissolved or worn away to leave a shallow cave. The bridge is only a few yards wide, but is one of the finest examples in England. The site also includes a section of river disappearing underground into a parallel shallow cave development and then resurfacing a few hundred metres further downstream. God's Bridge is on the Pennine Way.

God's Bridge. (By kind permission of Michael Seggie)

DID YOU KNOW?
There is a prehistoric stone circle just south-west of Lune Head Farm, near
Eggleston, which consists of six boulders forming an arc and is linked to other
outlying stones.

2. Fortifications

Stanwick Iron Age Fort

Though not strictly in Teesdale, this is a modern border, and as this complex is located on one of the main routes to the area its story is crucial to the surrounding region.

Around 3 miles from the Scotch Corner junction of the A1, and heading west on the A66, is a signpost directing you to East Layton on the B6274. After 3 miles down this road you come to a small village called Forcett, and still visible in the surrounding countryside are the remains of an enormous Iron Age settlement. To place this site in perspective, the well-known Maiden Castle in Dorset is 19 hectares (47 acres), whereas Stanwick Iron Age Fortifications cover an area of over 300 hectares (750 acres). This is comparable to the size of the nearby town of Richmond; the true scale of the complex is awe-inspiring.

What remains are a series of earthworks. These banks and ditches are still large in scale when you bear in mind the erosion and degradations that will have occurred in over 2,000 years. This would have been a mammoth construction project by what must have been a large populace of Iron Age people, using only picks and shovels. There are some estimates that give the potential occupation of the site up to as many as 85,000 people. This would be a large-scale project today, so the need for defence must have been very important and the suspicion is this was due to the Roman invasion.

Stanwick Fortifications.

Excavations carried out by Sir Mortimer Wheeler in the 1950s and subsequently by Durham University revealed timber roundhouses dating from around AD 50. They also discovered many luxury artefacts from around Europe – including Germany, southern France and Italy – which demonstrates a complex society who were trading with other people. It is believed the fortifications were occupied by the Brigantes – a tribe concentrated in the north of England and whose queen is recorded by Tacitus, the Roman historian, as Cartimandua. This British queen chose co-operation with the Roman invaders, which would explain the traded goods found on the site. It is also recorded that following another defeat, the leader of the resistance to the Roman invasion, Caractacus, headed north to seek protection from the Brigantes. But instead of helping the resistance leader, Cartimandua had him put in chains and handed over to the Romans. He was taken and paraded through Rome, where Emperor Claudius was so impressed with him that he was pardoned and allowed to live in Rome for the rest of his life. The Brigantes queen furthered her alliance with the Romans when she did not join Boudicca's (the other famous queen of the period) rebellion in AD 61.

Cartimandua is an interesting character and obviously a woman of great power in the north. How much of her story is true can only be gauged by Roman histories, but the next part of her story would not be out of place in a soap opera. She was married to Venutius, who was possibly a member of the Carvetti tribe from Cumbria, but divorced him and replaced him with his armour-bearer or charioteer. Venutius, obviously upset with this

The entrance to the English Heritage section of the embankment.

and her attitude to the Romans, did not accept the situation and raised support to attack his former wife. Even with Roman assistance, Cartimandua could not put down the revolt, and in AD 69 Venutius took advantage of a period of Roman political instability following the death of Nero and became leader of the Brigantes. Venutius was now king, but within ten years the Romans would defeat him and subjugate the region to push the boundaries of the empire ever north.

Many artefacts have been found during the excavations, including and Iron Age sword, a skull from a severed head with wounds inflicted by a sharp weapon, and a metal hoard – some of which is displayed in the British Museum. During the excavations in the 1980s the Durham University team found a male burial near a rampart and a horse's head had been placed upon the body.

Take the road to Aldbrough St John, where a signpost will direct you to a short path through a gate, and a short stroll on top of the monument leads to a reconstruction of part of the embankment and wall. This is where Sir Mortimer Wheeler excavated and rebuilt a section of the north-west defensive wall. Though it was not built to its full height, it does demonstrate how imposing the defences would have been.

There are other Iron Age forts nearby at Dalton, and in-between Wycliffe and Ovington there is the unusually named Cockshot Camp. Situated on a cliff above the River Tees, the fort covers around 4 acres and consists of two ramparts and a ditch. The tip of a sword was found during some work carried out within the camp.

Roman Forts and Signal Stations

As the Romans conquered the north of England, they employed the methods that had seen them create one of the largest and most influential empires in history. These methods are in evidence along the road from Catterick (Cataractonium) to Brougham (Brocavum) near Penrith and at many points in-between. These include temporary forts known as marching camps and more established forts at Greta Bridge, Bowes (Lavatrae) and Brough (Verterae). In-between these forts, including across Stainmore, are a series of signal posts to ensure quick communication along this strategic route. The Romans built their forts one day's march apart, so they were able to support each other quickly if under attack.

Greta Bridge Roman fort.

Above: Roman altars in the gardens of Rokeby Hall.

Left: Roman town at Piercebridge.

The conquest of the north is believed to have been carried out between AD 69 and AD 83 during the governorships of Vettius Bolanus, Quintus Petillius Cerialis and Gnaeus Julius Agricola. By the end of Cerialis' time as governor in AD 74, he had established Carlisle as a northern outpost in the west and Corbridge in the east. The troublesome Brigantes under Venutius are thought to have been quelled or pushed north by AD 71 and pacified over the following decade. Agricola pressed north using these northern bases to move into Scotland from AD 79, and reached as far north as the Dundee area. The years following AD 87 were used to establish borders and consolidate their gains. Watchtowers, forts and signal stations were built during this period as a means to subdue the population and secure their conquests.

One of the best examples of a Roman fort is sited at Greta Bridge, behind the Morritt Arms Hotel. You can imbibe yourself at the hostelry and access the raised earthwork through a gate in the beer garden at the rear. The large, raised oblong shape covered in grass is (with a little imagination) still visible as a fort and a number of alters and other Roman artefacts have been discovered over the years. One of the stones found was a Roman tombstone for a little girl with the inscription: 'To the shades of the departed Salvia Donata who lived eight years one month.'

From Bowes or Lavatrae the Roman road branches towards Barnard Castle (now the A67) and originally crossed the Tees at Startforth. While workmen were digging the foundation of a gasometer in July 1839 they discovered a section of this road.

Apparently formed of limestone rock placed edgeways and compacted with fragments of sandstone, the road headed up what is now Galgate, by Streatlam and Staindrop (through the Raby Estate) until it meets the Piercebridge to Binchester road.

There is evidence of Romano-British settlements in Upper Teesdale too, with sites at Ettersgill, Holwick and Newbiggin. Coins were found at the Bridge Inn at Middleton and it is known that the Romans exploited parts of the North Pennines to extract lead, silver and other minerals. Roman pottery was discovered at a native settlement at Forcegarth, and a horde of around a dozen Roman coins were found near High Force. This could, of course, be simply from the Romano-British locals trading with the occupiers, but it would be naive to imagine these resources were not controlled by a local force of Roman overlords.

Barnard Castle

The earliest evidence for prehistoric activity around Barnard Castle dates to the Bronze Age. A Bronze Age burial urn was found in the town, and a spearhead was found at Barnard Castle School in 1951 along with another on the banks of the River Tees in 1974, but there is no evidence for settlements during this period. The remains of any Bronze Age homes or villages are usually only identifiable by changes in ground markings, which make their discovery extremely difficult or incredibly lucky. The only known remains from the Iron Age (800 BC to AD 43) are two necklaces made from twisted gold wire. These were found in 1873 and are now in the British Museum, where they are described as 'a gold pen-annular bracelet made from a single circular section bar which has been unevenly curved. It was then forged at each end into bent-back conical shaped terminals.'

There are no remains of any Roman settlement in Barnard Castle, but there is evidence of a historical Roman crossing or ford at Startforth, whose name is a likely corruption of

Barnard Castle.

'Street Ford'. This ford has recently been upgraded to a likely bridge across the Tees and there is a plaque in place at the site of the old gasworks by the river. In all likelihood the bridge would have been protected with some kind of small settlement or fort, and Roman coins have been found in Bridgegate.

The Norman castle, from which the town takes its name, was probably originally a ringwork by Guy de Balliol around 1095. It was later fortified by his heirs Bernard de Balliol and Bernard II as a shell keep castle between 1130 and 1200. From the 1200s the Balliols were in the ascension when John de Balliol gained land and titles in Scotland through his marriage to Devorguilla of Galloway. This allowed his son, John de Balliol II, to become a contender for the vacant Scottish throne in 1292. Scotland was a continual problem to the English kings and when Edward I was asked to assemble Scottish and English lords to decide who would be King of Scotland to avoid a civil war, they chose John as the new king. He swore loyalty to Edward, but once in power rejected the authority of the English king. By 1296 this had resulted in Edward marching north with an army, John surrendered his right to the Scottish throne and was imprisoned in the Tower of London. All of his English estates were confiscated, although he was later allowed to retire to his family estates in Picardy. John, the English King of Scotland, was born in Barnard Castle and is thought to be buried in the Church of St Waast at Bailleul in France.

The castle was not maintained by subsequent owners including the Beauchamps and Nevilles, who regarded it more as a source of revenue. In 1569, during the Rising of the North – in which rebels planned to depose the Protestant Elizabeth I and replace her with

Barnard Castle from the book *Rivers of Great Britain* (1892).

the Catholic Mary, Queen of Scots – Barnard was besieged by 5,000 rebels. Sir George Bowes was unable to stop his men from leaving the castle and was forced to surrender. Following this siege the castle continued to fall into ruin. In 1630 it was sold to Sir Henry Vane, who used the castle as a source of materials for extensive improvements he was making to his main residence at Raby Castle, near Staindrop.

An interesting feature of the castle is the sally port just above the county bridge. A sally port is a gate or passage in a fortified place that was used by troops to make a sortie, and was named from the French *saillie*, meaning 'to come or jut out' or 'to leap'. This particular one would have been used to protect the important crossing over the Tees as and when needed.

Raby Castle

It is claimed King Canute (or Cnut) the Great first owned the Raby (or Rabi) lands and may have built a manor house on the site. Canute's deeds are told in Norse poetry and he was described as a ferocious Viking warrior who was 'tall and strong'. He became king of England and Denmark around 1016 and divided the country into four regions; Wessex was ruled directly by him, with East Anglia, Mercia and Northumbria ruled by his appointed representatives. Canute converted to Christianity and was acknowledged by the pope as the first Viking to becoming a Christian king. He ruled England for nineteen years, dying in 1035 and is buried in Winchester Cathedral.

After 1066 there was huge political upheaval following the Norman Conquest but Uchtred FitzMaldred (who was descended from Gospatric, Earl of Northumberland) became Lord of Raby, followed by his son Dolfin. Dolfin was born around 1110 at Raby and in approximately 1131 he is recorded as paying homage to both the king of England and Scotland when he was granted Staindrop and Staindropshire by the prior of Durham Cathedral.

He had a son called Maldred, the father of Robert Fitz Maldred who married Isabel Neville. Being from a great Norman family, Isabel would inherit the manors of Sheriff Hutton and Brancepeth. Robert, Lord of Raby, changed his name to that of his wife and it was stipulated by her family that all their sons were to assume the name Neville (Neuville in Norman).

Geoffrey de Neville, Baron of Raby (1197–1242) was the first true Neville to own Raby; this powerful northern family would continue to dominate the region, as well as politics, over the next 350 years. Nevilles were involved at the famous battles of Bannockburn (1314), Berwick (1319), Crecy (1346) and Neville's Cross (1346). During this period the family grew in prominence as Lords of the Marches and, along with the Percys, were regarded as 'Kings in the North'.

The present castle was built by John, 3rd Baron Neville, who obtained a licence to crenellate it in 1378, although this probably meant improving and adding to an already existing building. He was followed by Ralph, who was created the 1st Earl of Westmoreland in 1397 by Richard II following his support during an attempt by other lords to restrict the king's favourites. Within three years he had switched allegiances, helping the Lancastrian and his brother-in-law Henry IV obtain the throne and in return was named Earl of Richmond, a Knight of the Garter and Earl Marshal of England.

Raby Castle.

St Mary's Church, Staindrop.

His first marriage to Margaret Stafford produced two sons and six daughters; with his second marriage to Joan Beaufort, a further nine sons and five daughters were added. The youngest daughter was called Cicely and known as the 'Rose of Raby' because of her great beauty. She married Richard, Duke of York, and was the mother of two kings – Edward IV and Richard III – who held the Crown in thanks to their cousin, Richard Neville (also known as the 'Kingmaker').

Ralph Neville died on 21 October 1425 and is buried in the Church of St Mary at Staindrop, where, to commemorate him, there is a magnificent alabaster tomb with effigies of himself between his two wives. Despite this, neither of his wives is buried with him: Margaret Stafford was buried at Brancepeth, while Joan Beaufort was buried with her mother, Katherine Swynford, in Lincoln Cathedral.

Ralph was succeeded by his grandson – also a Ralph – who was involved in a long-running feud over the family estates. They were eventually ordered to keep the peace by Henry VI. Ralph was succeeded in 1484 by his nephew – another Ralph – because his father, John, was killed at the Battle of Towton in 1461 fighting for the Lancastrians. It is not known if Ralph, the 3rd Earl, fought in the Yorkist defeat at Bosworth and it is entirely possible that he was one of the northern lords who held back until the outcome was more certain. After the battle he entered into several bonds for his good behaviour, with £400 and 400 marks to the new king, Henry VII. On 5 December 1485, he granted the wardship of his eldest son and heir, Ralph Neville, to the king.

The Nevilles continued to be influential and were involved in battles with the Scots, including the intriguing Perkin Warbeck and his six-year masquerade as Richard, Duke of

Neville memorials in St Mary's Church, Staindrop.

York. Another Ralph was present at the Field of the Cloth Gold and was a signatory to the letter to Pope Clement asking for the divorce of Queen Catherine of Aragon.

The next few years were a disaster for the family, starting with Henry, 5th Earl of Westmorland, who took part as a boy in the Pilgrimage of Grace against the Reformation. He was a staunch supporter of Queen Mary Tudor, and the family continued to cling to the old faith. Henry's son Charles, 6th and last Neville Earl of Westmorland, and Thomas Percy, Earl of Northumberland, were leaders of the ill-fated rebellion known as the Rising of the North in 1569. The Earl of Northumberland was executed in 1572 but Charles managed to flee to Holland, where he died in poverty in 1601.

After the disastrous involvement in the Rising of the North of 1569, the castle and its lands were forfeited to the Crown. It was not until 1626 when Sir Henry Vane purchased Raby, Barnard Castle and the estate for £18,000. Sir Henry was a Member of Parliament and important member of Charles I's household – he was his governor and later his treasurer. He chose to make Raby his principal home and therefore de-roofed and removed stone from Barnard Castle to repair it. At the time many of the castles in the area were robbed by their owners to maintain the principal home and consolidate their holdings.

Vane helped create the deadlock that led to the dissolution of Parliament by Charles. In 1641 Vane helped bring about the impeachment and execution of the king's chief minister, Thomas Wentworth, the Earl of Strafford. As a result, Charles dismissed Vane from office. He ended up working for the Parliamentary cause during the Civil War, but was opposed to the death of the king in 1649. He continued to sit in Parliament, but because of opposition to their policies he actively participated less and less. His son, Sir Henry Vane the Younger, was a Protestant and governor of one of the newly established colonies until he became at odds with some of the rigid dogma of the religious groups. He returned to England, where he was involved in the Civil War against Charles I; however, he was also opposed to the execution of the king and was persecuted by the Cromwell dictatorship. In 1656 he was briefly imprisoned for publishing a pamphlet attacking Cromwell's protectorate and helped the army overthrow Oliver's son in 1659. Following the Restoration he was sentenced to death by Charles II and was executed in 1662 for his past Parliamentary activities. The king deemed him to be 'too dangerous a man to let live' and on the scaffold his speech was deliberately drowned out by trumpets and drums. He gave a paper copy of his speech to his friends for later publication before laying his head on the block and died 'as much a martyr and saint as ever man did', according to Pepys.

Christopher Vane succeeded Henry the Younger and was MP for County Durham from 1675–79 and for Boroughbridge from 1689–90. After the Glorious Revolution in 1688, where the Catholic James II was ousted from power, he was made a privy counsellor, and in 1698 he was created Baron Barnard of Barnard Castle by William III.

Henry, 3rd Lord Barnard, was created the Earl of Darlington in 1754 and restored the castle, with further work being carried out by his son in 1768. The 3rd Earl, William Henry, was created Duke of Cleveland in 1833 and his son Henry began another period of rebuilding in 1843. Over the next ten years he converted the south-facing round tower into the magnificent Octagon Drawing Room.

The Vane family still own the Raby estate, with the 12th Lord Barnard and his family still the incumbents of this glorious castle and jewel of the Dale.

Streatlam Castle

Streatlam Castle was a baroque stately home built around earlier structures (possibly as early as the thirteenth century) and later demolished by the Territorial Army following its abandonment. Owned by the Bowes-Lyon family, who were Earls of Strathmore and Kinghorne, the house was one of their two principal seats, alongside Glamis Castle in Scotland. The building was the playground of Elizabeth II's mother. After the First World War the Earl of Strathmore, rationalising his estates, chose Glamis Castle over Streatlam because he considered it, according to the 1915 edition of *Country Life Magazine*, 'awkward and unsatisfactory'.

Most of the estate was sold to private tenants, and the remainder made approximately £100,000 at auction. The house was gutted and in 1959 it was blown up as part of a training exercise by the Territorial Army. The gatehouses and park remain on the Bishop Auckland road just outside of Barnard Castle.

Scargill Castle

Scargill Castle is more of a fortified manor house with a settlement and associated field system. The house is thought to have been built during the twelfth century by Warren de Scargill while he was supervising the construction of Bowes Castle for Henry II. Some partial rebuilding work took place on it during the fifteenth century. It was thought that Edward II was entertained there when on a visit to Scargill in 1323, but later investigation suggests the visit mentioned in the rolls was actually closer to a residence near Leeds.

The last of the family line was Sir Robert Scargill, who died in 1530. He had two daughters, the eldest of which, Mary, married Marmaduke Tunstall of Thursland Castle in Lancashire and linked to the Tunstalls at Wycliffe and Hutton Magna. The building featured on Channel 4's *Time Team*, where medieval remains and a Tudor fireplace were uncovered as well as outer fortified walls.

Scargill Castle.

Bowes Castle

Built within the Roman fort called Lavatrae, the Norman castle at Bowes fulfils the same strategic role of its predecessor. To protect this important trade route over the Pennines has been the goal of many invaders to these shores. Even before the Roman invasion, this location was crucial in guarding the eastern approach to the Stainmore Pass and vital in combating raids from many different enemies.

Around 1136, Alan the Red, Count of Brittany, built a keep in the north-west sector of the old Roman fort. This pattern of recycling fort sites continues along the A66, with the medieval castle built within a Roman fort at Brough (Verteris) and Brougham (Brocavum). After the death of Alan's son, Earl Conan the Little, who died without male heirs in 1171, the ownership of the castle passed to the Crown. Henry II is responsible for strengthening a castle regarded as vital for the defence of the kingdom against a Scottish invasion, with most of the work being carried out between 1171 and 1174, including repairs made following an attack by the Scots in 1173.

In 1173 the castle at Bowes was besieged by William of Scotland, who retreated when Geoffrey, Archbishop of York, approached with a relieving army. No further expenditure on its fabric is recorded after 1187, and it appears to have remained under ownership of the Crown until 1233, when it was presented by Henry III to the Duke of Brittany. In 1241 the castle and manor of Bowes were given to Peter of Savoy, who was the king's uncle and also Earl of Richmond. Edward II subsequently granted the castle to John de Scargill in 1322, causing much local resentment. By 1325 the castle was already falling into ruin and again reverted to the Crown in 1471. By the seventeenth century it had become redundant, and after the Civil War parts of it were dismantled and the stone was reused for other buildings.

Bowes Castle.

Cotherstone Castle

Only earthworks now remain of Cotherstone Castle, which is situated high above the Tees near the Hagg. This fortress was erected under a licence of King John in 1200–01 by the Fitz Hughs. Little else is known of its history or when it became a ruin, but local folklore tells of a Scottish raid.

Left: The remains of Cotherstone Castle in 1870. (By kind permission of the Parkin Raine Trust)

Below: Cotherstone Castle from the Tees.

Barnard Castle, Garrison Town

Originally raised as the 3rd Regiment of the Durham Militia under Henry Vane, 2nd Earl of Darlington in 1759; the initial strength was 369 men headquartered at Barnard Castle. Over the years they served to protect the country in times of war, including during the French Revolutionary Wars when they were tasked with maintaining order, moving French prisoners and anti-invasion duties. The barracks sited off Birch Road and Wilson Street were erected in 1864, and are labelled on maps from 1894 as 'barracks (militia depot)'. The barracks were active during the First World War as the headquarters of the 4th (Special Reserve) Battalion Durham Light Infantry and were enlarged in 1914. The barracks were sold to the town in 1930 and the majority were demolished by the 1970s, but, much to the credit of the town, the ornamental gateway survived and is now Grade II listed.

On the south side of the River Tees is Her Majesty's Young Offender Institution (HMYOI) Deerbolt, and was once the site of Deerbolt Camp. Though information is a little scant on the beginnings of this army camp, the *Teesdale Mercury* reported as early as 1890 of the decision to hold the annual training of the 3rd Battalion of the Durham Light Infantry (Militia) under canvas on this site. They stated the troops would be supplied with water by the Barnard Castle Local Board of Health and also commented: 'I can see that the good people of Startforth have been tidying themselves up a bit to receive the military in a becoming manner. Soldiering and spank cleanliness are, or ought to be indissolubly connected.'

The camp was active in 1909–10, prior to the First World War, and was still tented at that time. In the Deepdale Valley next to the camp a series of ruinous ranges and buildings are still located. The ranges seem to predate the camp as it is known that the ranges were used for a shooting contest on New Year's Day in 1879. The challenge was won by Colour Sergeant Ainsley, who won 9*s* and a cheese. As a child I used to find spent bullets and very occasionally live ammunition; musket balls, powder flasks, rifle bullet casings from Martini-Henry rifles and several mortar-type shells have been found in the ranges area over the years. The Martini-Henry was first used by the British Army around 1871 and lasted for around thirty years. The ranges continued to be used until after the Second World War when the area would be closed to the general public.

Aerial photographs from the 1940s show a complex of buildings around a square had been established and used as barracks. One soldier called Norman Wood recollected it as 'brick built, single storey barrack blocks arranged in cul-de-sacs by Squadron. I was put into 251 Squad, B-Squadron and marched to what would be my home for many months to come.' He described the inside of the barracks as having 'double bunks with slatted timber bases and on this there was a paillasse which was filled with straw'.

During the Second World War, the camp was principally used by the 54th Training Regiment of the Royal Armoured Corps, who specialised in tank and vehicle maintenance and radio training. There are also records of the Special Forces using the base in the 1950s but the camp and ranges were eventually closed in 1972.

After the Miracle of Dunkirk in 1940, soldiers were distributed throughout the country and new bases were required to house these men. As Barnard Castle was a small town in the centre of Britain it was an unlikely target and generally out of the range of the Luftwaffe, therefore Stainton Camp to the north-east of the town was selected and

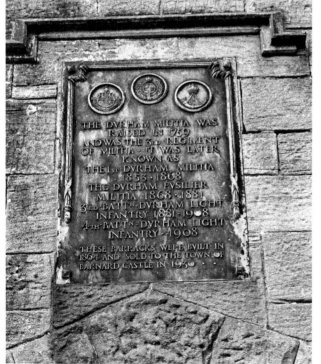

Above: Old barracks gateway.

Left: Plaque on the barracks gateway.

procured by the War Department in November 1941. The site was also used as a prisoner of war camp where the prisoners would be put to use on local farms.

The camp was used by the army until the end of the Second World War and remained in military use until the 1970s.

Other camps to the east of the town included Barford, Streatlam, Westwick and Humbleton. All were occupied during the Second World War, but were mainly decommissioned and demolished in the 1960s. Many of the troops trained in and around Barnard Castle went on to fight in Italy and were used on D-Day – the invasion of France on the Normandy Coast.

Brough Castle.

DID YOU KNOW?

There was a prisoner of war camp at Stainton Grove. The camp at Blackbeck, known to the Red Cross as No. 613 for German working companies, was located to the south of the main camp.

3. Places

Eggleston Bridge Chapel

Eggleston Bridge had a chapel located at the southern end that was founded by Thomas Newleyne, Rector of Romaldkirk. This was quite a common feature on bridges throughout Britain in the fourteenth and fifteenth centuries; they were often chantry chapels where prayers were said for the souls of the founders and benefactors of the bridge, and they also provided a place for travellers and pilgrims to attend Mass and pray for a safe journey.

The original bridge was built around 1450. As the chapel had been unused since the Reformation it was demolished when they built a new bridge in the seventeenth century. Very few bridge chapels survive today; examples can be found in Wakefield, Rotherham and St Ives.

Gardens at Eggleston Hall.

Crosshill Stone and Grains o' th' Beck

A wayside cross known as the Crosshill Stone is situated on a ridge just to the south of the farm at Grains o' th' Beck, beside the bridge crossing Arngill Beck on the Brough to Middleton-in-Teesdale road. The monument is made up of a socket stone and shaft and stands just over 1 metre high. There are signs of mouldings on the shaft and the structure is Grade II listed. It is the only known survivor of the wayside crosses marked for this route on John Speed's map of 1610. The other crosses were located at Laithkirk, Kelton and Stackholm.

Grains o' th' Beck is an interesting place, with the building being a farm that once operated as an inn. There was also a chapel-cum-school building and a post office. On the main building there is a flush bracket (a type of benchmark for Ordnance Survey) and a quern stone appears to be built into the wall. There is also a milestone painted white with black lettering, possibly from the turnpike of the 1800s. There used to be the Grains o' th' Beck Tup (Ram) Show and an annual fair, so travellers would camp here on their way to and from the local fairs.

The Grains o' th' Beck Meadows are also revered as a Site of Special Scientific Interest due to the flora and fauna, which includes some rare types even for Teesdale.

Crosshill Stone.

Grains o'th' Beck
quern stone?

Lartington, Chantry

In Henry V's Calendar of Patent Rolls there is a licence granted to Henry and Elizabeth Headlam to found a chantry in the chapel of St Mary at Lartington. The document, dated 25 May 1414, refers to a John de Laton (the parson of the church of Rumbaldkyrk), John Eppelby the Elder (chaplain), Thomas Soureale (chaplain), Robert Jakson of Castro Bernard (chaplain), and Henry Hedlam and his wife Elizabeth. The chapel was dedicated to Our Lady and in 1546 was valued at £5 6s 8d per annum. The building was recorded as still standing in the year 1620, but there is not a trace remaining today.

During the Pilgrimage of Grace – the rising against Henry VIII's break with the Roman Catholic Church and the Dissolution of the Monasteries in 1536 – a chantry priest of Lartington named William Tristram donned his armour and rode the countryside to rally support for the cause. He was accused of being one of the busiest priests in the cause of insurrection and was rebuked for being overzealous in bearing arms, raising money and encouraging parishioners to fight.

Kirkcarrion, Lunedale

One of the most intriguing features of the Teesdale landscape is the ancient monument known as Kirkcarrion. Situated around 2 miles to the south-west of Middleton-in-Teesdale on a ridge in Lunedale, this tree ringed tumulus or ancient burial ground is thought to be the resting place of a great chieftain called Caryn. The site has been known by different names such as Kirk Arran (according to an OS map from 1856) and Carreg Caryn.

Kirkcarrion burial mound.

Kirkcarrion seen from the heart of Middleton-in-Teesdale.

In 1804 a local farmer was taking stones from the pile to build an enclosure on Crossthwaite Common when a chamber or kist was uncovered. The chamber was formed from flat stones intentionally set on edge and covered by another large flat stone. When the cover stone was removed, a small cremation pot was found inside. The relics from the chamber were given to the landowner, Lord Strathmore, who took them to Streatlam Castle where they were put on display. Apparently there was another excavation carried out in the mid-1800s, but no records remain of what was found. Under instruction from Lord Strathmore, the site was partially repaired, a pine tree was planted to mark the spot and a dry stone wall was built to encircle the mound.

With so much disturbed archaeology the true story of the site may never be known, though the burial mound of Caryn still remains a mystical place and local folklore claims the site is still inhabited by the chieftain's spectre.

Prehistoric Carvings, Barningham

There are some stones on Barningham Moor that contain some of the most important prehistoric art in Durham. Some of the patterns used here are very rare, with ancient carvings on rocky outcrops and others carved onto freestanding boulders. A few are even found on smaller rocks that have been built into walled stone enclosures thought to date from the Bronze Age or Iron Age. The purpose of these carved rocks is unclear; one of the main theories is that they had some religious or ritual significance. There is also a number of probable Bronze Age burial mounds and even the possible remains of a stone circle near Osmaril Gill, which would have been of great significance to the local tribes.

St Michael's Church, Barningham

There is little evidence of Roman or early medieval inhabitation in Barningham apart from name of the parish itself, which in Old English probably means 'the village of Beorn's people'. This suggests there was a settlement here by the time the name was first recorded in the Domesday Book in 1086. It is believed the old Church of St Michael was built in the eleventh century, the site of which can be seen as a low platform just to the south of the present church, which was built in 1812. A fragment of carved twelfth-century stone has been built into the new church, and the remains of a number of medieval gravestones can be seen. One is for a rector called Thomas Messenger who died in 1394, another has two bears at the foot of a cross, and one is a coffin-shaped slab with an interlacing pattern of knotwork that could be Saxon in origin.

Newbiggin

The village of Newbiggin has been a settlement for at least a thousand years, but finds such as Mesolithic flint tools in the vicinity are evidence of much earlier occupation. Later in the Bronze Age and Iron Age they lived in small communities with roundhouses and walled enclosures, and it must be assumed these communities carried on into the Roman era. Although there is little evidence of Roman occupation in the area, it is well known that they exploited the local minerals. The name Newbiggin is actually from Old English, meaning 'new buildings or houses', which suggests a pre-Norman Conquest settlement.

In 1857 Fordyce described the village:

> The village of Newbiggin is situated on the north bank of the Tees, two and a half miles north-west from Middleton. It contains a small Wesleyan chapel, which is one of the oldest in the district, and in which the Rev John Wesley occasionally preached. There is a smelt mill and a few tradesmen. A former public house is now converted into a private dwelling.

Evenwood

Much of the old village of Evenwood has been lost due to the mining and general industrialisation of the area, which was followed by the 'restoration' of the environment after the industrial decline. The earliest evidence for settlement comes from the Mesolithic period – a number of small flint tools.

It is believed there would have been a Roman presence in the area as the old Binchester road is within a mile of the village.

The name of Evenwood in Old English means 'even or level wood' and suggests an Anglo-Saxon settlement, which is further confirmed by records of the village being given by King Cnut to the Bishop of Durham around AD 1000 on his pilgrimage to the shrine of St Cuthbert.

Some medieval buildings that no longer exist include an old stone tower or castle, though remains of a moat are marked on the Ordnance Survey maps.

Coal was discovered in the fourteenth century and the village is associated with the iron trade. During the industrialisation of the nineteenth century coal was worked throughout the area, with pits including Brockwell and Busty. There were 500 people employed in an industry with an annual output of over 400,000 tons a year. This industry declined after the Second World War and is no longer operational today.

The Red Well

Sat in its own enclosure in a field near the GSK factory is an ancient well that was once claimed to have had medicinal qualities; the Chalybeate, or Red Well, contained high levels of iron and other minerals. The spring used to leave a red stain on the stone and was a popular place to visit to take the waters, which was thought to aid the constitution or purify the blood.

It was in the nineteenth century when Dr George Edwards, with the permission of the then Lord Barnard, created walks through Flatts Wood, along Percy Beck and beside the banks of the River Tees. The intention was to offer the local workforce somewhere with fresh air and exercise away from the mills where they worked and the squalid conditions they lived in. The result of his work was the Cleveland Walk and the King's Walk, both beautiful strolls through a wooded valley that snakes its way via paths and wooden bridges. The Red Well was popularised by Dr Edwards, who encouraged the residents to make use of its health-giving properties and stated: 'its valuable laxative quality has, I know, been ascertained.' The walks still exist and are much used by the locals, but the taking of the waters from the Red Well is no longer recommended.

Coldberry Mine

It is estimated around 10,000 lead industry sites survive in England from the Bronze Age to the present day, but only 251 have been identified as being of national importance. The Coldberry site is among this small number.

Eggleston to Stanhope Road.

The Coldberry Gutter is considered to be the largest and most spectacular hush in the North Pennines. It is a gully or ravine excavated by use of a 'controlled torrent of water, to reveal or exploit a vein of lead or other mineral ore. Hushing may have derived from the Roman period on the continent and from the 16th century in England, but most surviving examples are believed to be of 17th to 18th century.'

Coldberry Mine is a landscape feature that is visible for many miles and is unusual 'in that it cuts through the watershed between neighbouring valleys'. Though the majority of the remains of the mine are from the nineteenth century, the site retains a number of rare and well-preserved features such as the 'water balance incline and round buddle'. There may also be further archaeological deposits in the area and the site is of particular importance because of its location in a diverse mining landscape.

Bowes

Bowes represents the beginning or the starting point for the ancient Stainmore Pass, which was an important route for the prehistoric inhabitants of the north. The area shows settlement from as early as the Mesolithic period (around 10,000 BC), with evidence of settlement at Ravock on the moor next to the Pennine Way, just north-west of modern Bowes. Settlement of the area continued up until the Bronze Age (2500 BC), which is evidenced by the large hoard of bronze objects found at Gilmonby: nearly thirty axes, thirty-seven spears, fourteen swords and many other items.

Bowes Church.

A spectacular Iron Age discovery was made in the nineteenth century when a hoard of gold necklaces was found, though unfortunately they have now been lost.

Into this world of indigenous people the Romans arrived, making use of this natural route across the Pennines. On the moor above Bowes (on the A66) there is a marching fort, which was probably used as they were conquering the north and also temporarily before locating to Bowes. Lavatris, as the Romans called the fort in Bowes, is at the junction of the strategic Stainmore Pass and road to Binchester, which was occupied from the second century to the late fourth century. The fort was originally built using large river boulders set in clay, faced with timber at the front and turf at the rear. It is around 143 by 133 yards and covers approximately 4 acres, with evidence of a settlement on the outskirts of the fort referred to as a vicus. A vicus was a civilian settlement, like a shanty town, that sprang up next to a fort. The fort would be the centre of trade and the vicus would provide services to the soldiers, usually including a brothel.

When the Normans conquered the north, they built a keep in the bounds of the fort (an early form of recycling) and maintained the strategic importance of the site. Bowes was an important staging point before or after the long climb up the bleak Stainmore Pass, with its inns hosting mail coaches and its blacksmiths preparing their horses. The route was also used to drive cattle and it was reported that the herds could be up to 4 miles long. At its peak in 1840 the village had a population around 1,000, but following the opening of the railway in 1861 and improved motor vehicle mobility this had dropped to around 600 by 1960. The village was bypassed in the 1980s and the population dropped even further to the current numbers of around 250.

RAF Bowes Moor

Just north-west of Bowes is the derelict RAF Bowes Moor (No. 81 Maintenance Unit), a base used from December 1941 to store mustard gas. The bombs were initially stored in the open under tarpaulins or in wooden sheds, and it is estimated that some 17,000 tonnes of chemicals were stored on the 564 acres of moorland. Apparently it was found that the sheep on the moor would eat or nibble at the tarpaulins and disturb the bombs. It was decided to improve safety and new buildings were erected to house the larger bombs. After the war the content of the stored bombs was disposed of, but some may have already contaminated the area. German nerve gases were also stored there on a temporary basis until it was shipped by train to the military port at Cairnryan, Scotland, and put onto old cargo boats to be sunk in the Atlantic. In 2007 the Ministry of Defence launched Project Cleansweep to check or clear up old munitions and chemical sites throughout the United Kingdom. The sites – including Bowes – have now been declared safe by the MOD.

The Old Well Inn

The Old Well Inn in Barnard Castle could be one of the oldest in town and possibly dates back to the twelfth century when the castle was built. The building has its own well and was probably used as a water source to brew beer for the castle.

The Old Well Inn was previously known as the Railway Hotel, but in the 1827 *Gazetteer* it was known as The Ship with a Jane Barker as the landlady. In 1877, when John Myers was landlord of the Railway Hotel, during the annual Durham Fusilier Militia Training,

The Old Well Inn.

some of the soldiers were billeted to the hotel. These troops were so unhappy with the conditions at the hotel they protested vigorously, and it led to two charges being brought under the Mutiny Act against Myers for not bringing the place up to standard when ordered by the military doctor.

The Old Well Inn has undergone a recent refurbishment and I am reliably informed the accommodation and welcome has greatly improved.

Whorlton Bridge

Whorlton Bridge was opened in 1831. It is a wooden-planked roadway supported by wrought-iron suspension chains and is the oldest suspension bridge in the country still supported unaided by its original chains. The crossing is restricted to one vehicle and is Grade II listed, but in late 1942 it was vital to the war effort.

Winston Churchill came to Barnard Castle by train on 4 December 1942 to witness preparations for the invasion of France and the bridge was being used for a mock attack by British troops. His visit was shrouded in secrecy, but some photographs were taken and the reported fifteen tanks protecting him as he resided at Humbleton Camp were a hint of the important visitor. Legend has it that when Churchill arrived at Barnard Castle he greeted the town's stationmaster with a handshake and the comment, 'My, you're a big bugger.'

There is an old army training video called 'The Fighting Section Leader', which shows the troops crossing the River Tees and making a mock assault on Whorlton Bridge. The bridge is clearly identifiable along with the nearby lido; the troops continue to bayonet sandbags and shooting at pop-up wooden cut-outs of German soldiers in the woods. The men finish with a drink in an unidentified pub, possibly The Bridge in Whorlton.

Whorlton Bridge.

The River Tees at Whorlton Lido.

Churchill by Whorlton Bridge in 1942.
(Image courtesy of the Parkin Raine Trust)

4. Events

Battle of Hunderthwaite

In the period following the Norman invasion, Teesdale may have been one of the most horrendous places to live in the country. The Normans were laying waste to the north following a rebellion in 1069 by a Danish king, Edgar the Aetheling, who had united with the local Anglo-Saxon nobles Edwin of Mercia and Morcar of Northumbria. This became known in history as the Harrying of the North after William the Conqueror had ordered the land north of York to be shown no mercy and for his army to crush the rebellion. The chronicler Orderic Vitalis commented:

> In his anger at the English barons, William commanded that all crops and herds, chattels and foods should be burned to ashes, so that the whole of the North be stripped of all means of survival. So terrible a famine fell upon the people, that more than 100,000 young and old starved to death. My writings have often praised William, but for this act I can only condemn him.

Taking advantage of the turmoil, Malcolm III of Scotland invaded via Cumberland and entered Teesdale to plunder the lands. The likely route taken was via the Stainmore Pass and down the Lunedale Valley until they came up against several English nobles at Hunderthwaite who were soundly defeated as they 'fell to the Scottish blades'. The Scottish army then split, plundering down the Tees Valley to attack Cleveland as well as Northumbria and Wearmouth.

The exact location of the battle is not known, but the description of 'hunderdeskelde' – which translates as 'Hundred Springs' – is thought to be Hunderthwaite. It is said Malcolm III ravaged the countryside and killed women and babies; though these statements are quite often simply propaganda, it may have saved William I from carrying out the same task.

By 1072 the rebellion had been crushed and William's position was once again secure, so he ventured north with an army and a supporting fleet. Malcolm was defeated by William in battle at Abernethy on the River Tay and he sought fealty, even handing over his son Duncan as a hostage. He also arranged peace between William and Edgar Aetheling. There were further incursions into Northumbria, but in 1080 William sent his son Robert Curthose north with an army while his brother Odo punished the Northumbrians again. Malcolm made peace once more, and this time kept it for over a decade.

Further disputes with the new Norman king, William Rufus, over the Cumbrian border led to more raids by Malcolm with his Northumbria allies. But he was ambushed while marching back to Scotland by Robert de Mowbray, Earl of Northumbria, near Alnwick on 13 November 1093. Malcolm is recorded as being killed by Arkil Morel, the steward of Bamburgh Castle, and the Battle of Alnwick also claimed the lives of Malcolm's son

Edward as well as Edgar Aetheling. Malcolm's body was taken to Tynemouth Priory for burial but may later have been removed and reburied at Dunfermline Abbey or Iona during the reign of his son Alexander.

A Time of Plague, Famine and Drought

The 1600s were a time of turmoil and upheaval for Teesdale and the rest of the country. In 1622 and 1623 the northern uplands were struck with a major famine; though the country had been wracked by famine before, this period was of particular note. Following a record poor harvest in 1622, the following year resulted in high wheat prices and low sheep prices, which led to famine in the area. The worst effects of this were felt in north-west of the country – Cumberland, Westmoreland and Dumfriesshire particularly suffered. There was also a significant rise in burials at this time – estimated to be around 20 per cent of the population. The situation was even desperate in parts of the lowland east of England; a Lincolnshire landlord reported how one of his neighbours had been so hungry he stole a sheep, 'tore a leg out, and did eat it raw'. 'Dog's flesh', he wrote, was 'a dainty dish and found upon search in many houses'. In parts of Cumberland and Westmorland there were reports of the poor men, women and children starving to death in the streets.

The Butter Stone on Cotherstone Moor.

There were further occasions of famine; for example, in 1671 it was noted 'if great quantity of rye and other grain had not come in at Newcastle and Stockton, undoubtedly we would have had a great famine in Westmorland and Cumberland, Bishopric, Northumberland, and the North Riding of Yorkshire.' The famine of 1623 can be regarded as the last great famine.

Disaster would further befall the area at the very height of the English Civil War – a time of great upheaval to the country. It is recorded that the plague arrived in Romaldkirk in 1644 and one third of the population died as a result. One resident mentioned as a survivor was Grace Scott, who built herself a temporary abode on the fell around a mile from the village; a farm built on the site later is still called Gracie's Farm.

Down the road at Cotherstone, on the moor road to Bowes is the Butter Stone. This is a stone with a dished top where people would leave money in a vinegar solution to pay for produce left by local farmers. This was to avoid direct contact between people in an attempt to reduce the risk of becoming infected. Barnard Castle is reported to have been a victim of the plague in 1636 and 1645 when 'that dreadful visitation again made great havock in the town and vicinity'.

River Tees.

Across the River Tees at Gainford was the village of Barforth. Little now remains of the old village, except for a ruined chapel, a medieval bridge and dovecote. The plague is often used to explain the village's demise, and there is a story that the inhabitants of the village threw the bodies of plague victims down a nearby long tunnel known as Hell Hole.

According to the diarist Christopher Sanderson, who was born at Barnard Castle in 1617, there was an 'extraordinarie drie summer' and a poor harvest in the year 1652. He noted it was so dry that even by the end of October many of the wells had little or no water in them and people could walk 'dry-shod' over the River Tees. Great portents occurred in this year such as an eclipse of the sun in March: 'I see stars betwixt ten and eleven o'clocke in the morning.' The eclipse was an event that foresaw the ruin of monarchy in Europe as well as changes in the law, at least according to Nicholas Culpepper, gentleman, and student astrologer.

Throughout the mid-seventeenth century, the Civil War between the supporters of Parliament and the supporters of the king was compounding the plight of the people. Though it seems Teesdale was not the scene of any major conflict, some nineteenth-century books mention Parliamentary forces using Towler Hill along the Tees as a base to bombard Barnard Castle. There is no evidence the castle was held by the Royalists, though this story persists throughout various publications and may have been copied from a dubious source originally.

Barnard Castle and Teesdale was, however, used as a stopping-off point or conduit for strategic troop movements, and in 1642 the Royalist Earl of Newcastle marched south into Yorkshire with a force of 8,000. Captain Hotham attempted to prevent the Royalists from crossing the River Tees at Piercebridge but, heavily outnumbered, he was driven back. The so-called Battle of Piercebridge could be described as more of a skirmish than a significant engagement.

During the Second Civil War in 1648, when Charles I negotiated a secret treaty with the Scottish Engager group and promised to impose Presbyterianism in England, there was a series of Royalist uprisings throughout the country and a poorly organised invasion from the Scots. There were no major battles, but instead a series of skirmishes. During this period a Major John Sanderson, who served in Colonel Lilburne's Regiment of Horse, kept a diary of his movements and a narrative of events. In late February he records that he and his troops were quartered in Barnard Castle before moving on to Richmond, then York, but returned to Barnard Castle a mere five days later to pay his troops. He states on 28 February: 'in the morning all my soldyers payd their quarters in Barnard Castle'. He stopped off in Barnard Castle again a few days later as he headed to Northumberland, then returned while his troops mustered in Staindrop. He continued to patrol in the north, regularly visiting Barnard Castle, and even stabled his racehorses there. In April he was at Gatherley Moor Racecourse, where he 'tooke his meare and let her ride' with some success, it would seem, as he then comments: 'Major Smithson wone the plate & my Meare came second'. Afterwards he headed to Caldwell.

For the next few months he supported manoeuvres in the north until a Scottish army, led by the Duke of Hamilton, crossed the border in July. The Parliamentarians were engaged in several sieges throughout the country and unable to prevent the Scots taking Carlisle. The Scots, around 12,000 strong, marched south in support of Charles. General John Lambert's

Parliamentary horse were based at Penrith Castle and, though not strong enough to fight the invaders, they would use their agility and skill to gain time until they could meet up with Oliver Cromwell. Lambert retreated ahead of the Scots down the Stainmore Pass. Appleby Castle fell on 31 July, but he continued to block their route into Yorkshire and prevent any link up with other Royalist forces besieged at Pontefract Castle. Sir Marmaduke Langdale's Royalist horse were unable to break through Lambert's cavalry screen and reconnoitre the situation behind his lines, so were unsure of what lay before them.

Major Sanderson records the advance of the Scots to Appleby as he headed to support and meet up with Lambert at Bowes. He then manoeuvred between Bolam, Piercebridge and Wycliffe, before ending up at Egglestone Abbey on guard. There is also mention of a standoff between Lambert and Langdale's horse troops at Gatherley, but Langdale backed off – probably with uncertainty at the size of the enemy before him. Sanderson continued to support Lambert and crossed into Yorkshire to meet Cromwell before heading to cut off the Scots in Lancashire. The Scots were strung out from Lancaster to Skipton and oblivious of the approaching Parliamentarian army until they finally clashed on 17 August 1648 at the Battle of Preston. The Scottish army was scattered and Sir Marmaduke Langdale escaped to Nottingham only to be captured while resting in an alehouse. The Duke of Hamilton surrendered to Lambert at Uttoxeter on 25 August. Sir Marmaduke Langdale was later brought to trial, found guilty of treason and beheaded at Westminster on 9 March 1649. At the end of this conflict Charles I was executed following a trial conducted by Parliament.

Holwick School Strike

According to the *Darlington & Stockon Times* in 1938 there was a strike in support of the Holwick village school, which the North Riding County Council decided was no longer practical. The parents and supporters vowed to put up stiff resistance to the closure, believing it was wrong for the children to travel the 5 miles down the road to Mickleton. Tommy Oliver of Romaldkirk was booked to take his coach to Holwick each school day to ferry the pupils to Mickleton and back, but on the first Monday there were no children to pick up – the children had all been kept at home. This situation continued every school day for six weeks.

The protest meetings were held in the Strathmore Arms, and some mothers said they were prepared to go to jail rather than give in. Fred Shield, chairman of the parish council, gave the strike his full backing and a fighting fund was set up, with George Bell of the Strathmore Arms as treasurer. Different ideas were put forward, including establishing a private school as the school got brilliant results and its attendance record was near perfect. There were enough children under five in the village to ensure pupils in future years, but as the council threatened court action against the parents their resolve began to weaken.

Some took their children over Wynch Bridge across the Tees to the Newbiggin School, and one morning Tommy Oliver found four children waiting to be taken to Mickleton on his coach. The end of the strike was in sight and soon all the children were accommodated elsewhere. The parents had fought a noble battle but the Great Holwick School Strike ultimately ended in defeat.

View from Holwick Scar back into Teesdale.

Holwick Scar.

5. Buildings

Egglestone Abbey

Egglestone Abbey is located on a steep-sided promontory at the point where Thorsgill Beck meets the River Tees. The abbey was established between 1195 and 1198 by Premonstratensian canons – an order founded in France in 1121. They adopted the rule of St Augustine as well as borrowing from the stricter Cistercians' rule. The founders of Egglestone were the de Moulton family, whose title passed to the Dacres by marriage in 1314. The first church would have been small and narrow, but around 1250 the building was improved to accommodate an increased number of canons. Apart from the church and the east range, little else is visible above ground, though more recently evidence of the gatehouse has been discovered.

The abbey always suffered from poverty, but it was especially so when it was attacked by the Scots around the fourteenth century, and after the Dissolution of the Monasteries the site was granted by the Crown to Robert Strelley in 1548. He converted the east and north ranges into a mansion and installed a kitchen in the west range. In 1770 Sir Thomas Robinson

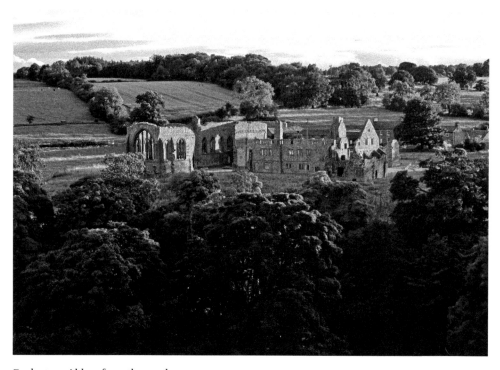

Egglestone Abbey from the north.

The packhorse bridge.

sold the abbey to John Morritt of Rokeby Hall. Morritt's descendant placed the ruins in the guardianship of the state in 1925 and later returned a notable collection of architectural stonework, including the tomb of Sir Ralph Bowes of Streatlam (d. 1482), which was re-erected in the church crossing. Below the abbey, just to the side of Abbey Lane, is the single-track seventeenth-century Bow Bridge or Thorsgill Packhorse Bridge.

Below Egglestone Abbey, next to the river, was a medieval corn mill that later became a paper mill. The paper mill was the subject of an 1818 painting by J. M. W. Turner, which portrayed the activity at the mill. In the sixteenth century there were two watermills and a fulling mill (cleansing of wool) linked to the manor of Egglestone, and from 1717–1807 a paper mill at Egglestone went with the manor. Thomas Girtin (1775–1802), a friend and rival of Turner, also painted the mill from a very similar place to him. The building also featured in Dan Cruikshank's BBC television programme *House Detectives,* and it is where my wife was born.

DID YOU KNOW?
At the coronation of George III, Sir Thomas Robinson of Rokeby was chosen to represent the Duke of Normandy and Aquitaine – the kings of England still pretended to own those provinces.

The Great East Window.

Section converted by Robert Strelley in the sixteenth century.

Bowes Hall

Not far from the castle is Bowes Hall, which was built in the seventeenth century by the Brunskill family. The family held the hall for six generations before it came under new ownership following the marriage of Anne Brunskill to Cornelius Harrison in 1766. In the early 1800s George Clarkson ran it as a boys' school, and it is thought Charles Dickens was inspired by the story of a murder at the house during his visit to Bowes in 1838.

The story is that George Clarkson came back from the Unicorn Inn, full of ale, only to find Wedgewood, the school usher, still awake in the parlour with some of the older boys. He lost his temper and, roused by the noise, Mrs Clarkson entered carrying a candlestick. A struggle ensued between Wedgewood and Mrs Clarkson, the candle went out and the room was plunged into darkness. When Mr Clarkson returned with another light he found his wife lying dead on the floor, bleeding from a wound to the head. Wedgewood was arrested, charged with murder and committed to York Castle; however, four months later he was acquitted because there were no credible – sober – witnesses.

Bowes Hall.

The Ancient Unicorn, Bowes

The local inn, the Ancient Unicorn, can trace its history as a coaching inn back to the sixteenth century and is reputed to be haunted by several ghosts, such as the Roman garrison who are said to return on the anniversary of a local massacre. In the churchyard is the grave of two locals named Edward and Emma, who have also regularly been seen. Their story is set in the eighteenth century and, due to the disapproval of their parents, the pair had to meet in secret. When Edward fell ill from a serious fever, he begged to see Martha and eventually the parents relented. Three days later he died and it is said Martha died shortly afterwards of a broken heart; the two were buried together in one grave. The event was commemorated in a ballad published in 1750 called 'Edwin and Emma' and also in the poem 'Bowes Tragedy', published around the same time.

Another ghost of a young boy has also been seen in the cellars of the hostelry, playing pranks on the owners and making noises or touching people.

St Mary's Church, Barnard Castle

St Mary's Church dates back to the twelfth century and was probably built at the same time as the castle. Alterations were carried out in the fifteenth and seventeenth centuries, and in the 1860s and 1870s major restoration was carried out including the rebuilding of the tower. Within the church is the effigy of Robert de Mortham, former vicar of Gainford, which dates to the mid-fourteenth century. Richard III was a benefactor of St Mary's

St Mary's Church, Barnard Castle.

when he acquired the town in 1474 following his marriage to Anne Neville. Richard made a grant of £40 for improvements to the church. The font dates to 1485 and is made from local Tees marble that is of exceptional size and quality. Octagonal in shape, it is sculpted on four of its alternate faces with a raised shield, each with its own symbol, the meanings of which are unknown.

Butter Market of Market Cross

At the junction of Newgate, Horsemarket and the Bank is the Market Cross. An octagonal structure built by prominent wool merchant Thomas Breaks in 1747. At various times the building has served as the Town Hall, a courtroom, lock-up and fire station but it was originally built to protect farmers' wives from the elements when selling their dairy products. The structure was not so popular and was blamed for getting in the way of horse-drawn traffic and for the putrid smells as it prevented the wind from blowing them away. The Market Place used to contain the old tollbooth (or Town Hall and courthouse) and shambles (or meat market), but these were demolished in 1808. It was realised that the shambles and piles of butcher's offal were the source of the rancid smells and the Market Cross was saved.

The weathervane contains two holes that were made in 1804 when two drinkers in the Turks Head argued over who the best shot was. One was a soldier called Taylor, the other a gamekeeper named Cruddas who worked for the Earl of Strathmore at Streatlam Castle. The holes suggest they were both good marksmen.

Above the entrance to Breaks Folly, as it was known, is a stone panel inscribed: 'THIS BUILDING WAS/ ERECTED 1747 AT/ THE EXPENSE OF/ THOMAS BREAKS, ESQ/ NATIVE OF THIS PLACE'.

Butter Market Cross.

Blagraves House

Blagraves House is on the Bank, and takes its name from the Blagrave family who lived here in the seventeenth century. There are many myths and stories linked to this house, not all of which have been proven. A ceiling on the first floor has a panel with the date '1672' and the initials 'WIB', which commemorates a marriage within the Blagrave family that year. Records show the house was given by Richard III to Joan Forest, whose husband Miles Forest (Keeper of the King's Wardrobe) along with John Dighton were reputed to have disposed of the two young princes at the Tower of London. In an extract from the rolls of Richard III, it states: 'Grant for life to Joan Forest, widow, to the King's servant, Miles Forest, and Edward her son an annuity of five marks from the issue of the Lordship of Barnard Castle.' On a south-facing wall there are the remains of a carved stone boar figure similar to that on the castle – a symbol of Richard III.

During the reign of Elizabeth I the house was used as an inn known as the Boar's Head. The vaulted cellars once housed a brewery, where ale was made using water drawn from the existing well. There is a tale that a passageway is said to lead to either Egglestone Abbey or the castle itself. If true, it would most likely be the castle as this would only be a dig of 200 yards, but Egglestone Abbey would mean dropping to the level of the river, crossing underneath and rising back up to the abbey.

Blagraves House.

The deeds date from June 1725 when Blagraves House was bought by the fishmonger William Tomlinson from Michael and Mary Coates who were weavers. The attic of the house was secretly used as a meeting place for the followers of John Wesley, and various religious tracts inscribed on the walls were discovered under plaster. A statue of Charles I can be found to the rear of the building, which was left from when Blagraves was used as a museum and was known as Cromwell House. The reason for the name Cromwell House is that Cromwell rested here during the English Civil War and met his commander General John Lambert in October 1648 on a return trip from the north.

On 18 February 1684–85 James II was proclaimed here. The justices present were Sir William Bowes, Mr William Robinson and Mr Sanderson: 'Several gentlemen dined at Blagrave's and their music consisted of two trumpeters with silver trumpets and four drums.'

The County School

The public school in Barnard Castle is one of the most famous schools in the north of England. The school was founded in 1883 at the bequest of the industrialist Benjamin Flounders. His ambition was to create a quality public school regardless of faith and at a fraction of the cost of the older schools. Originally the North Eastern County School, the name was officially changed in 1924 but is still generally known to the locals as the County School.

Former pupils include the pharmacologists Edward Mellanby and Joshua Harold Burn, the industrialist and politician Percy Mills, the poet Craig Raine, the fashion designers Giles Deacon and Patrick Grant, and the actor Kevin Whately.

The Bowes Museum

One of the most magnificent buildings in the north of England and yet totally out of character for the area is the Bowes Museum. The building was designed in the French style by the architect Jules Pellechet, set within landscaped gardens and purely for the purpose of housing John and Josephine Bowes' collection of artwork and ceramics. The collection inside is one of the finest in the north-east and is crammed with internationally significant collections of artwork, including paintings by Goya, Canaletto and Turner. The star of the show is the nearly 250-year-old automaton *Silver Swan*, a life-sized model made from silver with intricate detail, which moves to eat fish from a stream. The building also houses a fine collection of local archaeology and historic façades from lost grand houses. When you visit – and you should – ensure you also find the intricately decorated clockwork mouse.

John Bowes was the illegitimate son of the 10th Earl of Strathmore, who was a successful businessman and travelled to Paris in 1847 to explore his interest in the arts. It was here he met the Parisian actress Joséphine Coffin-Chevallier; they fell in love and were married in 1852. She was a talented amateur painter with an interest in many artforms including paintings, ceramics, furniture and textiles. Together they began to cultivate the idea of creating a museum to house their growing collection in John's ancestral home of Barnard Castle.

Joséphine laid the foundation stone in 1869 and said, 'I lay the bottom stone, and you, Mr Bowes, will lay the top stone.' As the building was being constructed they collected

The Bowes Museum is set in grounds complete with war memorials.

The Bowes Museum, built in the French chateau style.

thousands of items to fill the floors of their palace with the arts. But in 1874 disaster struck when Joséphine died of lung problems, aged only forty-eight, and John Bowes was so stricken with grief that he almost stopped collecting art. The building work continued, partly as a memorial to his late wife, and in 1875 the foundations of a Catholic chapel in Bowes Museum's park were laid with the intention of being the last resting place of Josephine and John. The chapel was only partly built due to objections raised by some trustees.

In 1877 John Bowes married another French lady – Alphonsine – but the marriage was not a success and ended in separation. In 1885 John Bowes died before he could carry out Joséphine's wish of laying the top stone; he was buried in the crypt at Gibside (an estate in Derwent Valley) next to his wife. Despite their deaths the project continued under the leadership of trustees and the Bowes Museum was finally opened to the public on 10 June 1892.

In 1927 the partly built chapel was dismantled and rebuilt just outside the grounds of the museum. The following year the bodies of John and Josephine Bowes were taken from Gibside in the early hours of the morning and interred under a marble slab in the precincts of the completed Catholic chapel near the Bowes Museum.

Mortham Tower

The Mortham Tower is situated on the Rokeby estate, to the east of Rokeby Hall and the River Greta. It is essentially a fortified manor house; it was built in the fourteenth century for protection and added to over the following couple of centuries. The first mention of the Rokeby family in Yorkshire is in the thirteenth century when Robert de Rokeby was granted lands by King John. The original home was deserted after it was destroyed by the invading Scots following the Battle of Bannockburn in 1314, so they built the Mortham Tower. The family would have prominent roles over the next few years: serving Edward III against the Scots; Sir Thomas Rokeby was involved in the Battle of Neville's Cross in 1346; and Richard Rokeby was a standard bearer at Flodden in 1513.

Another member of the family, Christopher Rokeby, was involved in a fracas at a horse race on Gatherley Moor and was assaulted by Christopher Neville, brother to Henry, Earl of Westmoreland. The earl had sent his brother, supported by 100 men, to kill Rokeby, but many of the gentlemen on the field came to his assistance, shouting 'a Rokeby!' and proceeded at once to deal hard blows upon the Nevilles. Thomas Rokeby, Christopher's father, an aged man and a justice of the peace, used his great influence to restore the peace saying, 'although it grieves me to see him bleed, that bleeds, yet peace, the peace'.

In 1610 the estate was sold by Sir Thomas Rokeby to a William Robinson of Brignall who was 'merchant of the Citye of London'. The estate is described below:

> From Greta Bridge along the Greta to the Tees, along the Tees west to a croft parcel of Rokeby vicarage, thence south to the town of Rokeby by the boundaries, thence between the kirk croft and the vicar's croft and west along the middle of the town green or town gate of Rokeby, thence west to the middle of the street leading from Rokeby to Bowes to the east of Rokeby Moor, thence south as far as the boundary of Brignall, then east to Greta Bridge.

Mortham Tower.

However, it seems the Rokebys continued to live in the parish as the baptisms of the children of Mr Christopher Rookeby are recorded in the early 1600s. An article in the *Teesdale Mercury* pondered this, proposing the Rokebys may have continued to live at Mortham Tower – their ancestral home – even after they had sold their land.

Remains of St Michael's Church

Less than 50 metres to the west of Dairy Bridge are the remains of St Michael's Church, which once served the Rokebys. The earthwork and buried remains includes the church, a socket stone for a cross and an associated graveyard. There are a number of marked graves, including a group of seventeenth- and eighteenth-century gravestones, a small tomb slab, and a twelfth-century coped tomb slab. Though Rokeby was mentioned in the Domesday Book, the earliest mention of the church occurs in 1204 when the advowson of Rokeby Church was given to Brian FitzAlan of Bedale by the Lord of Rokeby Manor, Robert de Rokeby. The lead roof of the church was removed in 1674 and replaced with slate. In 1740 Sir Thomas Robinson built a new church dedicated to St Mary the Virgin to the west of Rokeby Park and the old church became disused.

Rokeby Hall

The Robinsons were Parliamentarians and Thomas, son of William and a barrister, raised his own troop of horse at his own expense. Unfortunately, Thomas died in a skirmish near Leeds in 1643, possibly at the Battle of Seacroft or in the build up to the Battle of Adwalton. William is also thought to have been involved, but his place of death is recorded as Rokeby; he may have died as a result of wounds he received in battle.

Rokeby Hall.

Abbey Bridge.

Scott's Cave at Rokeby Park. (By kind permission of the Parkin Raine Trust)

The success of the family does not seem to have diminished after the Restoration, and between 1725 and 1730 Sir Thomas Robinson built Rokeby Park in the Palladian style of a villa with wings. He is also said to have erected an obelisk close to the Roman road in honour of his mother's memory. Sir Thomas was extravagant in his lifestyle and in his later years his increasing debts led him to sell the Rokeby estate. It was advertised for sale in 1765 and eventually sold to J. S. Morritt in 1769. Morritt undertook extensive modifications to the hall and grounds. The church at Rokeby (1778), the Abbey Bridge (1783) and Greta Bridge (1789) were also built.

Rokeby was inherited by J. B. S. Morritt from his father in 1791 and owned the place until his death in 1843. He was great friends with Sir Walter Scott and it was to him that Scott dedicated his epic poem 'Rokeby'. The estate has been under the care of the Morritt family ever since and is well worth a visit. Only open for a few days in the summer months, the building is filled with artistic treasures, some even under the scrutiny of French historians as being of historical importance. The house retains the feel of a home as well as being a fine example of eighteenth-century architecture and furnishing.

Hotels, Inns and Taverns in Barnard Castle in 1827
An 1827 edition of the *Gazetteer* lists a total of twenty-five hostelries in Barnard Castle. The population was around 4,400 at this time – much lower than it is currently. People must have drunk much more regularly to maintain these businesses, helped by market days and by annual military training when the hotels hosted the soldiers.

Hostelry	Landlord	Location
Angel	Thomas Tunstall	Marketplace
Bay Horse	Geo. Bell	Horsemarket
Black Horse	Jas. Wilkinson	Newgate
Blue Bell	Robinson Cornforth	Bridgegate
Boar's Head	Dorothy Coates	Thorngate
Burns' Head	Jas. Ferrier	Church Gates
Fleece	Michael Wouldhave	Marketplace
Freemasons' Arms	John R. Davis	Bank
Goliath's Head	George Wilson	Horsemarket
Half-Moon	John Dalkin	Marketplace
King's Head Inn	Ann and Jane Harrison	Marketplace
Lambton Arms	Mthw. Harewood	Bridgegate
Old Black Horse	Mary Richmond	Newgate
Old Cross Keys	Joseph Clifton	Galgate
Queens Head	Francis Shield	Marketplace
Red Lion	Parker Crossby	Marketplace
Rose & Crown Inn	James Donkin	Marketplace
Royal Oak	Thos. Alderson	Bridgegate
Ship	Jane Barker	Bank
Three Horse Shoes	Mthw. Hedley	Galgate
Three Tuns	Joseph Nevison	Newgate
Turk's Head	James Peacock	Marketplace
Waterloo	Benj. Sweeten	Marketplace
Wellington	Hannah Westwick	Bridgegate
White Swan	James Thompson	Bridge End

Dirt Pit Convent Chapel

In the township of Newbiggin, in the area where Friar House Farm is located, stood a chapel and convent called Dirt Pit (or Dor Peth) belonging to Rievaulx Abbey. Following the establishment of the Cistercian house of Rievaulx around 1131–89, the order was granted certain privileges and lands in Teesdale by the Baliol family in return for spiritual blessings. The Cistercians held pasture rights throughout the whole of Forest as well as a hermitage and vaccary in Ettersgill. Further rights were held between Eggleshope and Hudeshope, as well as arable and pasture rights at Middleton.

At the dissolution in 1540 an inventory gave the rentable value of the former lands of the abbot and convent in 'Tyesdale cum Middilton' as £11 9s 8d. It was listed as belonging to the grange of Friar House, with the tenant being Roger Baynebrige.

The Old Poorhouses

A parliamentary report of 1777 recorded workhouses at Barnard Castle (fifty inmates), Bowes (twenty), Eggleston (twelve), Gainford (twenty), Middleton (twelve) and Newbiggin (twelve).

In 1827, Barnard Castle's workhouse was recorded as being located on 'De Mains' (Desmense) with a Robert Lyons as governor. The John Woods map of the same year shows the poorhouse near the bottom of Thorngate, and the name Old Poor House Yard is referenced in later records.

Teesdale Poor Law Union came into being on 18 February 1837 and the Teesdale Union Workhouse in Barnard Castle was erected at the top of Galgate in 1838 from a Poor Law Commissioner's plan of a 200-pauper model. Most of the establishment is now demolished, apart from a building thought to be the infirmary block. On the advice of Walsham in 1837, the Teesdale Union was split between Middleton and Barnard Castle due to the 'great east-west length of this Union'. The Middleton building was located at the end of California Row according to old maps, and is now on the junction of the aforementioned and Jubilee Place.

DID YOU KNOW?

A 1777 parliamentary inquiry found there were 1,916 workhouses in England housing around 90,000 paupers.

Newbiggin Chapel

The last service was held in May 2017 at what is claimed to be the oldest functioning Methodist church in the world. In 1759 the land was bought by three of John Wesley's travelling preachers and four local lead miners for £5 with the intention of building a

Newbiggin Chapel.
(By kind permission of
Cynthia Mackenzie)

place of worship. The chapel opened in 1760 and was visited by Wesley in the summers of 1772 and 1784. On one occasion he commented, 'We rode through wind and rain to Newbiggin in Teesdale. Being but a poor horseman and having a rough horse, I had just strength for my journey and none to spare; but after resting awhile I preached without any weariness.'

The chapel was enlarged in 1860, renovated in 1987 and further repairs were carried out in 2003. But with its closure in May 2017, the future seems uncertain – perhaps someone will maintain the building as a museum for future generations.

Greta Bridge

The village of Greta Bridge is located on the old route of the A66 and consists of just a few buildings, including the Morritt Arms Hotel, which dates back to the late seventeenth century. There was originally a farm on the site until it was converted into the hotel and associated buildings there today. Throughout the seventeenth century, with the rise of the mail coach, Greta Bridge became the second overnight stop for the London–Carlisle coach. There were three inns in Greta Bridge, including The George on the bridge on the other side of the river, and the New Inn, which is now Thorpe Farm. Charles Dickens stayed at Greta Bridge, and in the novel *Nicholas Nickelby* it was the meeting point between Nicholas and Squeers.

The bridge there was built in 1789 by John Carr for John Sawry Morritt and has been described as a 'bridge of some beauty'. It is narrow with a semicircular arch 24 metres wide, and is believed to have replaced one of Roman origin. Greta Bridge has been the subject of paintings by Cotman, Girtin and many others.

Morritt Arms Hotel.

Greta Bridge. (By kind permission of the Parkin Raine Trust)

Rokeby old entrance before the bypass was built.

Brignall

The parish of Brignall lies on the south bank of the River Greta and is probably of Anglo-Saxon origin. It is believed to come from the Old English word *briggen*, meaning 'bridges'. The likelihood is that this refers to either the bridge lower down the river adjacent the Roman fort, or that Brignall was also a crossing over the river. The Domesday Book records this area as mostly being wasteland, but by 1265 it had been given permission to hold an annual and a weekly market. The village was larger than it is now and some distance away are the remains of a thirteenth-century church called St Mary's. The village shrank during the sixteenth and seventeenth centuries, and some of the earlier medieval buildings can be seen as earthworks.

Barnard Castle Railway Station Portico

Within the Valley Gardens at Saltburn is the Albert Memorial, but it was originally the grand portico to the original Barnard Castle railway station. Built in the classical style in 1854, the porch has paired Corinthian columns with support entablature and dentil pediment of the roof. In 1862 the Darlington & Barnard Castle Railway closed this station to passenger traffic being replaced by a new station. Henry Pease was a director of the Stockton & Darlington Railway and owner of the D&BC. He was working on the first phase of his plans for Saltburn as a resort to rival Scarborough, which included the Valley Gardens. In 1864 Messrs Shaftoe and Barry of York were appointed to relocate Barnard Castle portico to its current position. The monument was dedicated to the memory of Queen Victoria's husband Prince Albert, whom Pease regarded highly. The memorial is now Grade II listed and protected for posterity.

Barnard Castle railway station portico.

Guano Warehouse

An 1854 map of Barnard Castle shows a guano warehouse located at the junction of George Street and Ware Street. Guano is basically bird droppings used as fertilizer and was first imported from Peru around 1820. The building must have been constructed sometime between 1827 and 1854, but most likely at the same time as George Street, which was built around 1839. The building has since been built over by a row of terraced houses.

The *Teesdale Mercury* carried an advert for Peruvian guano in 1855 that was imported by Messers Antony Gibbs & Sons and was available at Thomas Caldwell's warehouse in Barnard Castle. By 1867 the number of suppliers had grown and the adverts in the local paper had significantly increased – probably due to the product's success after the improvement of production from the land. This did not stop people from trying to find cheaper alternatives, however, and in a letter from 1856 a Henry May from the Hope Nurseries near Bedale suggests the following:

About the middle of the month of May I procured from the gas works six gallons of ammonical water, or gas-tar water, or the water which floats on the surface of the tar. I diluted it in six times its amount with water from a pond, and applied it in the morning to about twenty square yards of the middle of a meadow field. The day turned out sunny,

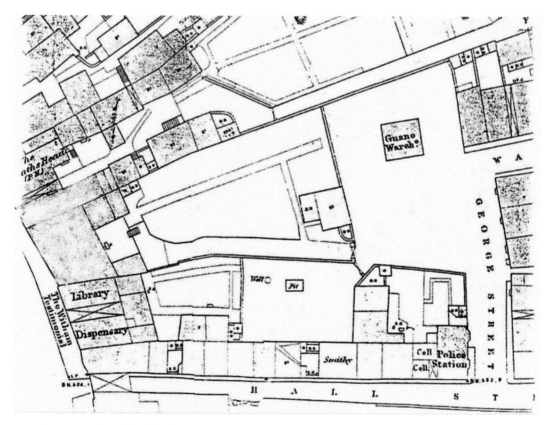

Guano warehouse location from an 1850s map.

and I went to look at the place in the evening, when lo! every blade of grass was scorched as brown as though it had been burned. I thought it was all over for seeing any farther what effect it had upon the crop. However, I chanced to go over the same place again this day, and to my surprise found the grass of a dark green, almost black, and as glossy and luxuriant as though it had been highly manured in the winter. I could tell to half an inch where the water had been put, and I consider that there is as much more grass. I can confidently assert that it will rival guano for grass and corn. If applied in a judicious manner. I think that it requires ten times its quantity of pure water to use it safely, and to be applied in the winter season, or in dull, showery weather; do not choose sunshine. If the water has so much of manuring principle in it, why not the tar itself and if mixed up with a compost, and applied in the winter, I think great benefit will be derived from it, but care must be taken to let it lie a few months before carting it on the land.

Tees Aqueduct

This 45-metre bridge across the River Tees was built in 1898 by the Thornaby-on-Tees engineers Head, Wrightson & Co. for the Stockton and Middlesbrough Water Board. It carries a major water pipe across the river and was designed to take water from upper Teesdale downstream to the towns and industry on Teesside.

Tees Aquaduct, also known as the Silver Bridge.

6. People

Benjamin Sweeten

Buried in the graveyard of St Mary's Church in Barnard Castle is a man who fought in the Peninsular War and the Battle of Waterloo, which culminated in the final defeat of Napoleon. Benjamin Sweeten was born in Barnard Castle around 1770 and at some point joined the Durham Militia, before joining the 52nd (Oxfordshire) Regiment of Foot. At the age of forty-three and described as a 'long serving member of the 52nd', he was appointed to the rank of quarter master. The hallmark on his silver shoulder belt plate is 22 April 1813; it was part of his uniform and was listed for sale online in 2017, along with his medal, for £13,750. His Waterloo medal with impressed naming to 'Quar. Mast. Ben. Sweeten, 1st Batt. 52nd Reg. Foot.', which has the original adapted steel clip, together with a newspaper cutting relating to the Sweeten Family and a later card box sold for £4,600 in 2017. The regimental history states he was present at the actions of Vittoria, Pyrenees and at the action above Vera, Nivelle, Nive, Orthes, Tarbes and Toulouse.

According to folklore he was originally 'pressed' into the navy, and on his eventual return he told stories of women dancing in the streets of Spain or Portugal with flowers in their teeth. It is also mentioned that when he was released from the navy in some port in the south of England, he spent two weeks walking back home to rejoin his family. Records show the 52nd being instrumental in the final defeat of Napoleon at Waterloo: their manoeuvre led to the breaking of the French Imperial Guard, and the pursuit that led to the French abandoning the field.

Benjamin Sweeten's Waterloo medal.

In 1816 he was placed on the half-pay list, and in 1833 he is still mentioned in the army list as QMS on half pay. In 1817 he married a Sarah Softly – she was described as a spinster and he a widower. The 1827 *Gazetteer* lists Benjamin as the landlord of the Waterloo Inn and a child born to a Benjamin and Sarah Sweeten in 1830. Benjamin would have been sixty years old by then, but this event would suggest there was still life in the old soldier.

His gravestone is inscribed with the following:

Here lie deposited the remains of Benjamin Sweeten late Quartermaster in His Majesty's Fifty Second Light Infantry Regiment and husband of Sarah Sweeten his surviving and disconsolate widow who in return for the great years of happiness she enjoyed during their union caused this stone to be erected as a tribute of love and affection to his departed worth. He ceased to be mortal at Barnard Castle December 13th 1832 in the sixty third year of his age.

Benjamin Sweeten's grave.

Frank the Hermit

Teesdale hermit Frank Shields was one of the most interesting characters in the Dale and he has a colourful history. Frank is believed to have been born in 1815 and baptised at St Mary's Church. Though little is known about his early life, he is supposed to have been a stable boy and post boy at the King's Head and is rumoured to have served in the military. There is a record of a Francis Shields receiving a military pension and it may be that he returned to his home town in his thirties without any accommodation.

In 1851 he was living in the round tower of Barnard Castle, where he fabricated a stove with a chimney and made stone seats. A contemporary account describes the main items of furniture as a table and seats made of stone, which served as Shields' bed at night. He obviously tried to make a home of his 'cell', with the walls adorned with a Native African spear and shield with some medals on display. This again hints at a military past, with the most likely conflict being the Anglo-Ashanti Wars, which took place in West Africa and may account for his whereabouts before 1851. During his time at the castle he managed to live by growing and selling vegetables as well as giving guided tours of the castle, often thrilling his audiences with historical monologues on its history. He became quite well known, which was partly thanks to the editor of the *Teesdale Mercury*, who was a regular visitor and gave front-page column to 'The Hermit of Barnard Castle' in 1857. One of his most celebrated visitors was the author of *Alice's Adventures in Wonderland*, Lewis Carroll (aka Charles Lutwidge Dodgson) who had connections with Croft-on-Tees and Stubb

Photo of Frank Shields, the Barnard Castle Hermit. (By kind permission of the Parkin Raine Trust)

House near Winston. He reported that Frank's tour was delivered in a monotone voice and without a break. He also saw Frank's home, watched him eat and tend to his garden. Perhaps this event was an influence when writing the famous book he published only a few years later.

Another visitor accompanied by two ladies paid him a visit and, on entering the cell, Frank was eating an 'enormous plateful of boiled beef, and evidently with a gusto that bespoke the keen relish known to few but the ploughman or huntsman. With a flourish of his knife which resembled a Scimitar – Frank bade us walk in.' When he had finished his meal he gave the impression of 'a man at ease with his stomach and the world'. He would then enter into conversation with the visitors and was considered 'a bit of an historian and a philosopher'. It seems he was rather irreverent to his 'landlords' too: when talking about 'lords and dukes' Frank said, 'I'se a better fellow than any o' them. What wad they do wid out their servants and their retainers, why, there isn't yan o' them knaws how to cuk his awn dinner!'

In 1861 he is recorded as a resident of the Teesdale Union Workhouse on Galgate and in 1871 as a general labourer in the Goliath's Head Inn, Horsemarket. Frank must have still occupied the castle throughout this period as it is understood he left it sometime around 1874, only to make Egglestone Abbey his 'new' home. He tried to return the abbey back to its original state – or at least his idea of it – and continued to give his historical tours. By then he was around sixty years old and solitude had made him more cantankerous with anyone who would stray onto his home. He was known to rise like an angry dog if disturbed or would chase people covered in a sheet to scare them off – possibly being responsible for the local myth of a mad monk.

In 1876 when the Bowes Museum was still being built, Frank decided he would like to investigate the building and proceeded to mount the main staircase to the roof. Mr Kyle, who was the chief clerk of the works, managed to talk Frank away from the roof, but apparently he grabbed Mr Kyle by his whiskers and set off up the stairs again. Other workers managed to stop him and he was led from the site to the Market Cross, where the town guardians took him into the care of the town. He is recorded in the 1881 census as inmate of Barnard Castle Poor Law Workhouse as a 'Gardeners Labourer (Dom) and Lunatic'.

Frank's demise came while frequenting The Burns public house, situated at the top of the Bank; he apparently slipped on the stone steps and was found dead the next day. The Barnard Castle Hermit, Frank Shields – or 'Frankie' as he was known to the locals – deserves his moniker as the last custodian of the castle and 'Duke of Teesdale'.

I think this quote from a gentleman called Walter White is splendid and describes a romantic notion of the man, he had heard 'that he had been crossed in love and that notwithstanding his lonely solitude he would go out at times and find a friend, and make a night of it'.

Lewis Carroll
Lewis Carroll, aka Charles Lutwidge Dodgson, lived in Croft-on-Tees from 1843–50 when his father, Revd Charles Dodgson, was Rector of Croft and Archdeacon of Richmond. It is believed some characters in the book *Alice's Adventures in Wonderland* were inspired by carvings in Croft Church. A branch of his family supposedly lived at Stubb House near Winston.

The old window from the Middleton-in-Teesdale medieval church.

Lewis Carroll visited Frank the Hermit at Barnard Castle around 1856 but didn't publish his first draft of *Alice's Adventures in Wonderland* until 1864. It makes you to wonder if he visited after the trip he described below, where he was less than kind about Bowes:

> We set out by coach for Barnard Castle at about seven, and passed over about forty miles of the dreariest hill-country I ever saw; the climax of wretchedness was reached in Bowes, where yet stands the original of Dotheboys Hall; it has long ceased to be used as a school, and is falling into ruin, in which the whole place seems to be following its example - the roofs are falling in, and the windows broken or barricaded - the whole town looks plague-stricken. The courtyard of the inn we stopped at was grown over with weeds, and a mouthing idiot lolled against the corner of the house, like the evil genius of the spot. Next to a prison or a lunatic asylum, preserve me from living at Bowes!

George Emerson Vipond

I noticed an unusual tombstone in the graveyard of St Mary's in Middleton-in-Teesdale, which has the name Vipond. Partially lost, the inscription remembered a George Emerson Vipond who served as a private with the 38th Battalion, the Eastern Ontario Regiment of the Canadian Infantry. He was killed in action aged thirty-eight on 2 September 1918 – only a month or so before the end of the First World War – and is buried in Dury Mill British Cemetery, France.

The son of William and Jane Vipond, he was born in Middleton-in-Teesdale on 2 January 1884. He moved to Great Tew in Oxfordshire where he was a student farmer at Tracey

Gravestone of George Emerson Vipond and family.

Farm, and also served for a few years in the territorial Queen's Own Oxfordshire Hussars. In 1904 he married Margaret Richards and they moved to Walcot Farm in Charlbury (as a tenant farmer), where they had a son and daughter. On 18 January 1912 he boarded the SS *Minnewaska* at Southampton bound for New York, leaving his wife and children behind in Charlbury. He lived at Hawthorn Farm, Libertyville in Illinois, where he worked as a coachman. In July 1917 he travelled to Toronto to enlist in the Canadian Expeditionary Force. He joined the 58th Battalion in the field on 29 March 1918 and transferred to the 38th in early August 1918.

He was killed in action between Arras and Cambrai during an assault on the village of Dury. Dury was behind the German defence system known as the Drocourt-Quéant Line, but on 2 September this line was broken by the Canadian and XVII Corps when Dury village and the hill just south of it were captured.

The graveyard is full of Viponds, who seem to have a long association with the Dale. Records show a Cuthbert Vipond was born in Middleton-in-Teesdale in 1634 and had a son called John in 1660.

Stan Laurel

Stan Laurel was born Arthur Stanley Jefferson in Ulverston, Cumbria, in 1890, but from the age of six was brought up in the north-east. He lived for a while in North Shields and attended Gainford Academy, King James I Grammar School in Bishop Auckland, and finally King's School in Tynemouth.

John Wycliffe remembered in the church.

Gainford Academy, located on the Green, was founded in 1818 by the congregational minister Revd William Bowman and remained at this building until 1899 before moving to North Terrace. It is most likely that Stan boarded when the academy was at North Terrace.

Stan's career flourished after he started in music halls and became Charlie Chaplin's understudy for a short while. He left for the United States and acted in silent movies, before teaming up with Hardy. Laurel and Hardy went on to become one of the most successful comedy acts of all time and made over 100 popular films.

DID YOU KNOW?

Thomas Edward Witham, who took over Lartington Hall in 1844, was regarded as someone who enjoyed the good things in life. He was a man who kept a good cellar, yet he had the village inn closed down.

John Wycliffe

John Wycliffe was the man who first translated the Bible into English and may be related to the Wycliffe family from the village on the Tees of the same name. He was an early critic of the Roman Catholic Church in the fourteenth century and his rebellious followers became known as Lollards.

Born in the 1330s, Wycliffe was a theologian at Balliol College in Oxford. Unconvinced by the Roman Church, he preferred a church of the spiritual rather than the physical. Much like an early form of Protestantism, he wanted the Church to be reformed and its wealth removed. John Wycliffe is sometimes known as the 'Morning Star of the Reformation' and his Wycliffe Bible (a translation from the traditional Latin into the common language) was completed by 1382.

Ironically, John Wycliffe died while he was at a Roman Catholic Mass in the parish church of Lutterworth, Leicestershire, on 28 December 1384 – he suffered a stroke and died three days later. Just over thirty years later, in May 1415, a papal council declared Wycliffe a heretic and it was commanded that his books be burned and his remains exhumed. In 1428 at the command of Pope Martin V, his remains were dug up, burned, and his ashes thrown into the river at Lutterworth.

Wycliffe Church.

The Tees at Wycliffe,
close to the
location of J. W. M
Turner's painting.

Eric Bloodaxe and Rey Cross

On the rise from Bowes to the summit of Stainmore, there is a worn down stone monument called Rey Cross. Legend has it that this is the burial place of Eric Bloodaxe, though it is also argued that the monument is simply a boundary stone for the border between Scotland and England. When excavations were carried out in 1989 no evidence was found of a burial; however, in all likelihood the monument is not located in its original place and is thought to have been moved during the widening of the road in the twentieth century. The monument is positioned in a layby very close to the summit of Stainmore.

Eric Bloodaxe was a colourful figure from the time of the Vikings and reigned for a short time as King of Norway and twice as King of Northumbria around the mid-900s. Eric is supposed to have become King of Norway after the death of his father and, in trying to maintain his grip on the Crown, had four of his elder brothers killed. He was eventually overthrown by his younger brother and sailed across to England, where he became King of Northumbria and used York as his base.

Rey Cross monument on Stainmore.

Stainmore.

The Norse sagas and the Anglo-Saxon Chronicle describe Eric Bloodaxe as being a bloodthirsty tyrant who was renowned for his cruelty and thuggish behaviour. They record the Northumbrians choosing Eric Bloodaxe as their king in AD 947 and the Anglo-Saxon King Eadred responded by invading and devastating parts of Northumbria. As Eadred's army returned south to Wessex, Eric's Viking forces caught up with its rearguard at Castleford and killed many of its warriors. Eadred threatened to destroy Northumbria, but the Northumbrians rejected Eric and accepted Olaf (a Viking from Dublin) as their ruler. This enraged Eric Bloodaxe, who responded angrily and took over Northumbria for a second time until, in 954, he was expelled again and King Eadred of Wessex regained control.

The legend is that Eric Bloodaxe was killed in an ambush on the bleak moors of Stainmore by Maccus, who is thought to be son of Olaf, the king from Dublin. The Norse sagas inform us that Eric was accompanied by five kings from the Hebrides and two earls of Orkney when he was ambushed. It is believed Maccus was acting on behalf of Eadred, who was using the established tactic of setting one Viking leader against another. The death of Eric Bloodaxe on Stainmore in 954 brought an end to independent Viking rule in Northumbria and the lands would then be ruled as part of England by kings in the south.

Captain Augustus Frederick Cavendish Webb

Within St Mary's Church there is a memorial to Captain Augustus Frederick Cavendish Webb, who was fatally wounded during the Charge of the Light Brigade in the Crimea. He died in 1854, two days after the amputation of his leg at Scutari (the hospital made famous by Florence Nightingale), and is said to have only received limited chloroform during the procedure. Just twenty-two years of age, he was the youngest son of Frederick Webb Esquire of Westwick. Apparently Captain Webb was found 'amid the carnage of Balaclava, his shin shattered and unable to ride'. Sergeant Berryman, who was recovering after having his second horse shot from under him, lifted Webb and brought him up the valley to safety. Like a scene from a film, Captain Webb was said to have greeted a colleague 'as if he had been injured on a football field' before the surgeons amputated his leg.

Sergeant Berryman was awarded the VC and a section of his citation reads:

On the 25th October 1854, on the plains at Balaclava, he would perform the actions which would lead to the award of his VC. Berryman was in one of the front two lines of the charge, and watched as Captain Nolan, who led the charge, was killed by a Russian shell. Berryman made it to the Russian guns, where his horse, wounded and with a broken leg

The Webb memorial in St Mary's.

could go no further. He himself was also wounded, as was his own troop officer, Captain Webb, whose leg was shattered and unable to ride. Unable to advance, they were joined by another 17th Lancer, John Farrell, and disobeying Webb's orders to save themselves, they carried him under heavy fire towards their own lines. With the help of a third man, Corporal Joseph Malone, from the 13th Light Dragoons, they got him to safety.

Saving Private Smith

Barnard Castle has its very own *Saving Private Ryan* story, which involves the Smith family who lived in Bridgegate. The story hit the national press during the BBC 100-year anniversary of the start of the First World War and was originally picked up by the local newspaper, the *Teesdale Mercury*.

Over two years, Margaret Smith lost five of her children: Frederick (twenty-one), Robert (twenty-two), George Henry (twenty-six), Alfred (thirty), and John William (thirty-seven). Wilfred, the youngest boy, was brought back home after an appeal by a vicar's wife to Queen Mary in the hope of ending the anguish of this already-grieving family. Wilfred went on to raise a family and died in the late 1960s. The decision to bring Wilfred back to his family is almost unprecedented and there may only be one other known case.

Abraham Hilton

On a cool afternoon in October 1902, a hearse passed the Kings Head Hotel, followed by eight mourning coaches containing the domestic servants, executors, personal friends, tenants and neighbours of the deceased. The procession passed through the town as a 'dumb peal' of the bells was rung from St Mary's Church. Hundreds lined the route as they passed down the Bank to Bridgegate, with the poor men and women stood especially reverently, anxious to pay their last respects to the memory of one who had helped them many a time in life. The cortege passed through to Lartington and further on to Cotherstone, where a large body of mourners awaited the arrival. The hearse stopped as close as possible but the coffin was taken a few hundred yards still to the grave, around which approximately 200 mourners had gathered. The coffin was of plain oak and there was a simple inscription on the breastplate: 'Abraham Hilton, died October 1st, 1902, aged 87 years.'

He was said to have been born in a thatched cottage in Bridgegate on 15 April 1815, though this fact was debated at length after his death and it was ascertained that Mr Hilton was in fact born in the last house of the Grove in Galgate. At that time the four houses above and below King Street had not built, and there was a field called 'Gip Gap' from Grove Park to Mr Hilton's garden. It was thought that the Bridgegate house was his mother's.

Abraham Hilton was a man of great philanthropic nature but Nonconformist in his beliefs, and was once quoted as saying: 'If the church spent less on pomp and circumstance and more on helping the poor, the world would be a much better and happier place.'

Abraham was a man of his convictions and set up various charities, including the Bowes Cross Charity and the Three Chimneys Charity, which still continue to this day as the Hilton Charities. They still provide services for the prevention of poverty, especially to the elderly in the Barnard Castle area.

As a young man he was labelled as being 'of delicate health' and because of this it is said he would go for a 4-mile walk every morning along the Barnard Castle Moor road and round by Broomielaw, before returned to the town. Apparently he would take his exercise in all weathers, even when there was snow, and he 'always ate his porridge and milk'. There is also mention of him and his friend George Brass going into Flatts Wood to build tree houses and only coming down at meal times.

His ancestry has been linked with the old baronial family called Hylton, who held great sway in the north of England and one branch had the manor of Hilton, which still stands near Staindrop. The family may have held the appointment of steward of the manor of Barnard Castle for a time and adopted a business as spirit merchant in the town. One member of the family was in the habit of bathing every morning in Percy Beck, even breaking ice to take a refreshing plunge; the *Teesdale Mercury* of 1902 says the pool was still known then as 'Hilton's Hole'. One of his ancestors was Cuthbert Hilton, a Bible clerk who married people on the County Bridge and was described by his contemporaries as the man that 'used to entangle certain sons and daughters of iniquity into an illegal marriage upon Barnard Castle bridge, in the middle of the river, between the County Palatine of Durham and Yorkshire, where the Lord Bishop's writ does not run'.

He succeeded to property and an old established business as a tea dealer and spirit merchant, in which he was well known from South Durham to the Yorkshire Dales. At the funeral was a Mr John Myers, who had the Masons' Arms at Witton-le-Wear, where Abraham used to stay when travelling for business, but he was equally well known in Swaledale and the Vale of Eden.

Not only was he industrious in business, but he was interested in science and philosophy. He was an amateur printer, painter and blacksmith, but also played the violin and was at one time the leader of the Barnard Castle Choral Society. Abraham was described as a man of purpose with 'no other object in view than the good of his fellow-creatures' as well as being a keen observer; he was diligent and hard working.

His house still stands in Galgate and is honoured with a blue plaque. He was a man of great charity who would help his fellow man, throwing pennies to the children or feeding the starved. It was reported to his maid, who stood at the bedside, that this courageous and undaunted debater lovingly whispered, 'Mary, are you there? Don't leave me', as his last breath.

Matthew Bendelow

Matthew Bendelow was born in Auckland, County Durham, in 1895 and not long after the start of the First World War he enlisted for the Yorkshire Regiment. He was sent to Gallipoli in 1915 and then on to Egypt. Gallipoli was a particularly brutal conflict and the Yorkshire Regiment suffered high casualty rates – a very difficult first posting. In July 1916 he arrived in France and following action near the Yser Canal in late September, Matthew was severely wounded. He had suffered from gunshot wounds to the left knee and left shoulder, and was reported as being seriously ill in a telegram to his wife. Due to his injuries his leg had been amputated above the knee, and his left shoulder had lost a lot of muscle. Luckily, he survived and was sent back to Richmond, until he was discharged as unfit for active service in May 1918.

He returned to the colliery where he had worked at Shildon for a short time before taking a position as auxiliary postman, sub-postmaster and telephone exchange superintendent of Bowes in 1921. He retired in 1961 after forty years' service to a community, where six days a week – in all weathers – he would deliver the post, pick up the papers and man the telephone exchange. His round was a 9-mile circuit on crutches and included a section on stepping stones over the River Greta. He was also a prizewinning rabbit breeder, billiard player, shoemaker, chimney sweep, Bowes' castle keeper, a cartoonist, poet and cook.

Private Bendelow Regimental No. 18407 of 6th Battalion, Alexandra, Princess of Wales' Own (Yorkshire Regiment) deserves our remembrance for his service during the war and his service to the community thereafter. David Charlesworth, Royal Mail historian and former Barnard Castle Delivery Office manager, specifically singled out Matthew's story for inclusion within this book as one of the many brave individuals with links to Teesdale who served in the First World War.

Matthew Bendelow on his delivery route. (By kind permission of Dave Charlesworth)

DID YOU KNOW?
To avoid being labelled cowards, a 'War Badge' was issued to service personnel to show they had been honourably discharged due to wounds or sickness from military service in the First World War.

Lieutenant Robert Alexander Morritt, 17th Lancers

Robert Alexander Morritt of Rokeby and educated at Eton and Sandhurst was commissioned into the 17th Lancers in May 1898. He was with C-Squadron of the 17th Lancers under Captain Sandeman, who were ambushed by the Boer Commando of Commandant Smuts on 17 September 1901 at Modderfontein. They were surrounded and outnumbered, suffering three officers dead, twenty-nine killed and forty-one wounded – including Morritt. It is believe he was shot trying to escape on a horse after the main engagement. Lieutenant Colonel Haig (later Field Marshal Haig of the First World War) was commanding the regiment at the time.

7. Aircraft Stories

Sptitfire Pilot, Startforth Church, Canadian War Grave

During the Second World War, on 1 March 1942, a Supermarine Spitfire was attempting to land near Dent House Farm (around a mile north-west of Brignall) but unfortunately crashed and killed the pilot. Apparently the Spitfire had flown up from low down by the River Tees, then climbed before swooping down over Abbey Lane where his sweetheart, Jean Norton, was playing tennis – she cheered and waved as he zoomed past. The pilot was Albert Lawrence Logan from the Royal Canadian Air Force based at Catterick and though the official reason for him being in the area is not known, he was almost certainly trying to impress his girlfriend from Startforth. It is believed the pilot had blacked out and had come round just before he was about to hit the ground. He died from a head

Grave in Startforth Churchyard.

✠ P O A L Logan

Left: Albert Lawrence Logan RCAF pilot officer. (By kind permission of Veterans Affairs Canada)

Below: Startforth Church.

wound caused by the gun sight as the Spitfire collided with the ground. Following his death, permission was granted for him to be buried at Startforth Church and his grave was tended by his young lady for many years after.

Albert was born on 21 October 1919 at Georgetown and enlisted just before his twenty-first birthday in 1940. He trained with the Royal Canadian Air Force at Dunuville, Ontario, and was promoted to pilot officer in December 1941.

Hampden, Barningham Moor

During the Second World War, on 5 October 1940, the crew of a Handley Page Hampden took off from RAF Cottesmore, Rutland, to carry out a night-time navigation exercise. The crew of four became lost in poor visibility and, as they descended through cloud to try and work out their position, the aircraft crashed into the ground near How Tallon on Barningham Moor. This high land is located around 10 miles south of the A66 road, where the aircraft had crashed through a dry stone wall and caught fire. The crew managed to escape the wreckage to await rescue, but one of the crew had broken both his legs in the crash.

Sepecat Jaguar GR1, Startforth

On 6 August 1981 a Sepecat Jaguar crashed into a field and farm on Startforth Park, 2 miles south-west of Barnard Castle. The Jaguar is an Anglo-French jet attack aircraft, originally used by the British Royal Air Force and the French Air Force in the close air support. The aircraft was operating out of RAF Lossiemouth, but 31 Squadron's home base at the time was actually RAF Bruggen in West Germany. The pilot did not eject and was killed, with the likely cause officially being disorientation in bad weather. The pilot was later named as Squadron Leader Roger Martin Matthews. The family at the farm were reported to be injured too, and the compensation included for damage to fields and hedges as well as one dead bullock. I was actually staying in Startforth that morning and never heard a thing, but it could have been a lot worse if it had flown another mile or so.

Messerschmitt Bf110

On 15 August 1940 a Messerschmitt Bf110 was shot down by a Spitfire flown by Flying Officer Ben Bennison from Catterick and crashed in the fields adjacent to the railway at Broomielaw. This twin-engine long-range German fighter was extremely successful in the early conflicts of the Second World War, until it came up against the Spitfire and Hurricane. Its lack of manoeuvrability against single-seat fighters was its downfall during the Battle of Britain. The worst day for the Bf110 was 15 August 1940, when nearly thirty were shot down.

Local man Alan Byde remembers the incident and explained,

I was twelve at that time and I can remember the plane burning, or rather smouldering. There was a smell of acrid fumes and the rear cockpit of the plane had twin machine guns mounted on a scarff ring. The ammo was stored in large pouches each side of the cockpit and because the plane was set afire when it landed, the heat kept the guns firing, spraying trees a field away. I was crouched in a sunken lane with other kids and we watched the trees shuddering with MG fire until the magazines were empty.

The usual armament of a Bf 110 included 20 mm cannon and 7.92 mm machine guns firing forward and aft. Alan remembers the heat affecting the cannon shells too as they 'exploded with a quiet thump' and with an army camp so close to Broomielaw at the time he recalled:

> Three men hurried across to be first on the scene but the German crew had set fire to the plane and the three men looted the plane of the radio, inflatable dinghy and other items. They stashed their loot but were apprehended and gaoled ... an army Lieutenant was stood on the unburned wing and got our attention. He had a shot in his hand, as there were several lying about and the boys were picking them up as souvenirs. He was very anxious and asked us politely, if we would please bring our souvenirs to him? The Lieutenant ended up with a small collection of shells at his feet.

The German airmen lived and were prisoners of war until they were returned to Germany after the war ended.

Royal Jockey, Ettersgill

On 20 June 1939, a British-American Air Services de Havilland Dragon Rapide aircraft had been chartered to fly John Crouch to Gosforth Park Racecourse in Newcastle. He was a jockey employed to ride George VI's horses and he had set off from Heston in West London to ride at Gosforth Park.

The aircraft had been seen in the York area, but failed to arrive at its destination. That evening the BBC broadcast an appeal for sightings or information, and the RAF made an aerial search for the missing aircraft – without success. It was on the next day that two men from Forest-in-Teesdale, the newsagent and postman, spotted the burnt-out wreckage on a hill called Dora's Seat just to the north of Ettersgill. The bodies of the three men – pilot, wireless operator and passenger – were located in the vicinity of the wreckage and taken to Moor House Farm on a hay sledge.

The inquest recorded a verdict of misadventure and no blame was attached to the pilot, but it was said he had lost his bearings and flown into the side of the hill. Ironically, had he gone just a few more feet to one side he would have cleared it.

John Crouch had been due to marry, but instead of his marriage his funeral took place at the very same church in Epsom. There were wreaths from the king and many famous racing figures of the time.

8. Amazing Tales

Medical Practices

Thomas Gyll of the estate at Barton in the North Riding of Yorkshire noted a rather curious cure for his cousin's condition in 1752. He refers to a method administered, saying 'he was electrified on his lips and cheeks' by a surgeon called Mr Dixon from Barnard Castle and he was then able to speak some words that he had not been able to do since he was 'deprived of the use of his tongue by a fit of the palsy on the 19th May 1751'. The words he was able to speak were 'how, saw, so, no, yes, as, was, me'. He hoped further treatments of electricity would fully restore his speech. This is a really early use of electricity in medicine and Mr Dixon must have been a modern-thinking fellow. Electrical charge could only be stored by the invention of the Leyden jar in 1745 by a German experimenter called Ewald G. von Kleist. He discovered it by accident while experimenting with electricity and although he did not understand how it worked, what he had discovered was that the jar was capable of temporarily storing electrons. It was only three years after the invention of the Leyden jar when doctors in Geneva began to treat patients with electric shocks. It was a Swiss physician who reported that victims of paralysis could sometimes be cured by repeated shocks to their muscles. As such, Teesdale is recorded as using these methods very early in their inception.

Treasure Found at Thwaites Hall

In March 1784 it was reported that some workmen turned up the turf of an ancient pasture at Thwaites Hall, Cotherstone, and found a leaden jar containing English coins cut in halves and quarters. These pieces of silver were said to date from the time of Henry I

Church of St Romald, Romaldkirk.

Hugh FitzHenry's tomb in St Romald's Church.

(1100–35) and this horde had probably been buried in the ground for over 600 years. Had the owner buried the coins to protect his wealth from raiding Scots or local feuding lords and been killed before he could retrieve his wealth?

Weather

19 September 1729

There was a very violent thunder and lightning storm in 1729 when a barn filled with corn caught on fire and burnt to the ground. An adjacent house in Startforth was also struck, which caused damage to the walls and furniture. A child was thrown onto a bed some distance away by the force of the strike but was said to have 'received no further injury than the fright.'

September 1824

In September 1824 there is a record of a storm in Teesdale, and one of such force it sent a 'tremendous flash' down the chimney of the poorhouse in Barnard Castle (the poorhouse was located in Thorngate). The strike came out of the fireplace on the first floor, past some old men sitting around the fire, preceded to the next room and tore plaster from the wall, ripped up some boards, then passed under an old woman in bed. The flash dropped to the lower level and 'played around the room with an astonishing manner leaving marks of its power' before going through a wall to the kitchen where it knocked a man down. The fireball passed out of the back door, having left a scene 'past description'. One person was left a little deaf for a while and the mistress of the house with a young girl 'only found the effects for a few hours'. The master of the house, investigating the building and checking on the elderly, found 'the smell of sulphur almost too much to enter some rooms'.

25 August 1832

On this day Teesdale was hit by a violent thunderstorm that was accompanied by a severe whirlwind. A thatched cottage was completely unroofed and left the occupants knocked 'senseless on the floor'. A large stack of hay was lifted and thrown down, and a man employed in breaking stones on the road was lifted off his feet and thrown to the ground, but 'without being much hurt'. The whirlwind crossed the Tees, tore up some large trees near Lartington Hall and killed a calf in a field at Cotherstone. The River Tees flooded to a great height and the road between Barnard Castle and Bowes was rendered almost impassable.

13 October 1839

It was reported during the night of 13 October 1839 that there was a 'strong gale of wind, accompanied by heavy and continued rain'. This caused the River Tees to swell above its usual height so much that the floods inundated many of the houses in Bridgegate. The floods were so severe they swept away furniture, clothes and other possessions.

Wycliffe Murders

In the fifteenth century this peaceful place by the River Tees was the scene of a double murder with one of the crimes committed by the parson of Wycliffe Church. It was early in 1482 when Roland Mewburne, parson of the church of Wycliffe, 'waylaid Robert Manfield with a knife and pierced his heart so that he died'. According to Durham Records this murder was for some reason pardoned by the king. But before too long James Manfield, a relative of the murdered man took his own vengeance and struck Roland Mewburne with a 'wallych bill' (Welsh bill – a cutting tool or weapon) who died from his wounds. This story became renowned as Manfield sought sanctuary from the church following his vengeful killing.

A Melancholy Case

It was New Year's Day morning of the new century in 1900 when a Mr Nixon, the relieving officer (an official appointed by a parish to administer relief to the poor) for the Barnard Castle district, was completing his rounds. He called at the dwelling of Margaret Dalston in the Well Yard at Barnard Castle to pay the local relief monies but the door was fastened and he could not gain admittance. The police were called and the constable forced the door, only to find a shocking spectacle before him.

The charred remains were lying in front of the fire grate and was badly burned. The poor woman had apparently fallen out of a chair in a fit. Her head was underneath the grate, and the upper part of the trunk was consumed to a cinder. The impression was

Miss Dalston had fallen with her hands enveloping her head. Dr Sevier was sent for and at once pronounced her dead. None of the neighbours had smelt burning in the yard, and it was speculated that the terrible occurrence had happened the previous night. There were no signs of a struggle and as the rug had only being shoved away around a foot, it was regarded as evidence of the poor woman's falling.

Miss Dalston was seventy-three years of age and lived by herself. She was seen alive the previous night, around 8 p.m., when she appeared in good health.

DID YOU KNOW?

Sir Henry Vane gifted his fire engine to the inhabitants of Barnard Castle in 1748 after a fire broke out at the home of Robert Newby and destroyed two houses before being extinguished.

Cholera

In St Mary's Churchyard, Barnard Castle, there is a memorial to remember the 143 people who died of cholera in 1849. The outbreak in Barnard Castle was so severe it is mentioned in the *Newcastle Guardian* on 15 September: 'At Wrekenton, Howdon, Walker, Seaton Delaval, North Shields and Barnard Castle it has been remarkably severe'.

St Mary's Church, Barnard Castle graveyard.

The disease struck fear into the heart of the populous. This dread was exacerbated because it was unknown how it spread; one explanation was a 'bad miasma' or poor air quality. At the time Barnard Castle was an industrial centre and the workforce was housed in cramped and dirty tenements. There were many families crowded around small yards or alleys, using the same toilets and drinking water. The disease ravaged the town and people were dying at such a rate that they were buried in a common grave.

There were several public health Acts passed around 1848 due to the national cholera outbreaks, but it was not until a York-born physician called John Snow traced the source of an outbreak in Soho, London, in 1854. It was his findings that inspired fundamental changes in the water and waste systems of London. This knowledge was then used to make similar changes in other cities in Britain and eventually around the world.

Barnard Castle Ships

SS *Barnard Castle* was an iron steam screw collier, built in 1878 in England by Laing James & Sons Ltd (Sir James Laing & Sons), Sunderland. The ship is known to have carried grain and cattle between Liverpool and New York, and apparently coal from England to the Near East. In 1879 the *Barnard Castle* ferried troops and supplies for Chile in the war against Peru. She came to British Columbia in 1881 and took coal from the city of Nanaimo to San Francisco. The ship hit Rosedale Reef on 2 November 1886 but managed to limp to Bentinck Island, where it eventually sank.

Another ship named HMS *Barnard Castle* was a 'Castle Class Corvette' before being converted to the rescue ship *Empire Shelter*. It was launched on 27 March 1945. She became an accommodation ship after the war along with *Empire Comfort* in Holy Loch, and was later an army transport in the Mediterranean. She was eventually scrapped on 29 July 1955 at Antwerp.

Fatal Railway Accidents

It was reported that on 8 December 1873 George Pearson from Shildon died in tragic circumstances on the railway. He was an engine driver and taking a heavy mineral train from Barnard Castle to Tebay when the accident happened at Cat Castle Bridge near Lartington. It was in a cut where a water spout crosses the railway and it is believed George was knocked down by this spout when walking over the engine tank, falling onto the rails where seventeen laden mineral trucks passed over his body. His head was found in the 'five-foot way', and his body between the rails, completely cut in two. In strange circumstances, his house door key was also found near his body cut in two and his pocket knife was crushed flat. He was conveyed to the Unicorn Inn at Bowes to await the coroner's inquest, which returned a verdict of accidental death.

These kinds of accidents were not uncommon in the early days of rail travel and only ten years later, almost on the same spot, George Gibson, a quarryman at Cat Castle Quarries, met a similar fate. He was in the space between the adjacent tracks, leaning on a shovel and watching the approach of a mineral train from Tebay. But he did not hear the fast goods train coming from behind him and was thrown onto the tracks, where several waggons passed over him, completely severing his head from his body.

Laithkirk Church.

Holwick Hunting Lodge.

Strathmore Arms at Holwick.

Overlooking Barnard Castle from Startforth.

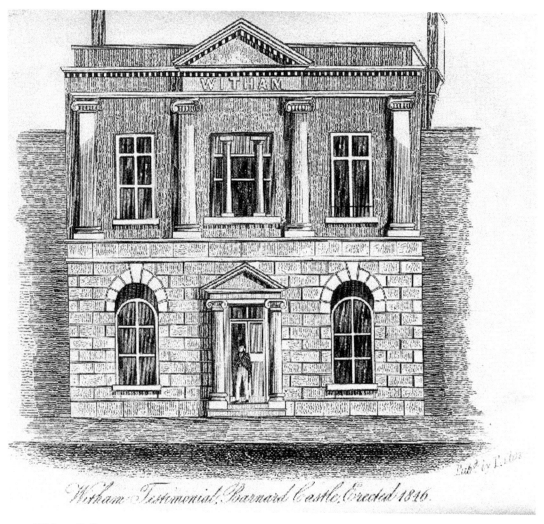

WITHAM

Witham Testimonial, Barnard Castle, Erected 1846.

Witham Hall.

On 29 July 1910 a passenger train from Darlington to Tebay on arrival at Lartington station ran into from the rear of another engine, which had become uncoupled. Apparently six passengers and the guard were slightly injured. Further problems occurred on this section of track on 15 December 1911: a freight train derailed when the driver braked too severely and, to compound the problems, a steam crane overturned during the recovery operation.

Kirk Inn, Romaldkirk, visited by Wainwright on his Pennine journey.

Tan Hill Inn – Great Britain's highest inn.

The paddling pool on the Scar Top in the mid-1960s – taken by my father.

About the Author

Andrew Graham Stables was born in the centre of Barnard Castle. He moved to Lartington before he was five years old and attended Cotherstone Primary School. He studied at Teesdale School, and is a member of English Heritage and a regular contributor to several online local history groups. His previous books include *Secret Penrith* (2016) and *Secret Kendal* (2017).

Acknowledgements

Thank you to my wife, Gillian, who is also from Teesdale. Many thanks go to the publishing team at Amberley, Gary Marshall for some photographs from the Parkin Raine Trust, Elaine Brinton, Cynthia Mackenzie, Alan Byde and Dave Charlesworth.

Select Bibliography

Blacker and Mitchell, *Egglestone Marble in York Churches* (1998).
Fordyce, *History of Durham* (1857).
Gazetteer of Durham and Northumberland Vol. 1 (1827).
Hutchinson, William, *History of Durham* (1823).
Lawrence, Danny, *The Making of Stan Laurel* (2011).
Major Sandersons War (2008).
North Country Diaries (1910).
Pigot's Directory (1828, 1834).
Sanderson, Frank, *Life and Times in Victorian Weardale* (2012).
Wilkinson, *Barnard Castle, Historic Market Town* (1998).

www.british-history.ac.uk
www.lunedaleheritage.org.uk
www.staintongrove.com
www.teesdalemercuryarchive.org.uk
www.workhouses.org.uk